TABLE OF CONTENTS

GW00538138

Satterley Vergin Associates
June. 1993.

PRODUCT DESIGN 5

Joe Dolce

Library of Applied Design

An Imprint of

PBC INTERNATIONAL, INC. ✦ NEW YORK

Distributor to the book trade in the United States and Canada:

Rizzoli International Publications Inc.
300 Park Avenue South
New York, NY 10010

Distributor to the art trade in the United States and Canada:

PBC International, Inc.
One School Street
Glen Cove, NY 11542
1-800-527-2826
Fax 516-676-2738

Distributed throughout the rest of the world:

Hearst Books International
1350 Avenue of the Americas
New York, NY 10019

Library of Congress Cataloging-in-Publication Data

Dolce, Joe.
   Product design 5 / by Joe Dolce.
     p.   cm.
   Includes index.
   ISBN 0-86636-185-5
   1. Design, Industrial.   I. Title   II. Product design
five
   TS171.D636   1992
   745.2--dc20   92-10433
                                    CIP

CAVEAT—Information in this text is believed accurate, and will
pose no problem for the student or the casual reader.
However, the author was often constrained by information
contained in signed release forms, information that could
have been in error or not included at all. Any misinformation
(or lack of information) is the result of failure in these
attestations. The author has done whatever is possible to
insure accuracy.

Color separation, printing, and binding by
Toppan Printing Co. (H.K.) Ltd. Hong Kong

Typography by
Jeanne Weinberg Typesetting

10 9 8 7 6 5 4 3 2 1

An Interview with Emilio Ambasz

by Joe Dolce

Emilio Ambasz—industrial designer, architect, landscape and graphic designer—was born in Argentina in 1943 and completed his undergraduate and Master's degree in Architecture at Princeton University. From 1970–76, he curated the Design department of the Museum of Modern Art, and among his notable exhibitions was "Italy: The New Domestic Landscape" in 1972. He has served two terms as the President of the Architectural League, won many awards in both architecture and industrial design, and has been the subject of several international exhibitions. In 1976 he designed (in collaboration with Giancarlo Piretti) the Vertebra chair, the world's first automatic, articulated office chair, which Mario Bellini once praised as "the reference point for everything that has been designed in its field since." His major building is the Lucille Halsell Conservatory in the San Antonio Botanical Center in Texas. He currently heads his own firm, Emilio Ambasz & Associates in New York City.

JD: The Eskimos have the igloo, the Greeks have the vase, and the American Indians have the teepee—If objects are the mirror of the society, what object best typifies the eighties, an era that's come and gone?

EA: The tiny 3-inch TV. Wasn't it Pascal who said, Consume, ergo sum? There it stands in one object, fetish and temple.

JD: Is design more about comfort or convenience or art?

EA: Mostly it's a prosthetic device, a device that makes up for something you don't have. If the world were a welcoming place, you could just put your hand on the ground, and take what you want; but since the world is not like that, you need devices to correct the deficiencies. Ideally, the object has to have some magic—it must please the mind and the heart. For me a product is usually a temporary reconciliation between one's desires and the difficulties which are imposed on us by the evironment. So in any product you'll find a tiny instance of peace and then a slowly eroding doubt about its construction and the longing for the next one.

JD: Was the Vertebra chair born out of vast study, or in a minute's inspiration?

EA: It wasn't that I sat down to design an office chair. I was simply sitting on one and rocking on two legs. I thought it would be good to have a chair that, much like a good friend, wouldn't give in to everything I say, would pose a certain resistance, and provide a certain amount of support. That was the birth of the tilt-back mechanism. I hit upon an idea, but not by any process of organized, analytical, deductive thought.

JD: Do you align yourself more with the artist or the engineer?

EA: I am interested in building products that provide a mechanical service, so I don't really think of the object artistically. I think of it more as a little animistically endowed entity that has a capacity of answering back to certain movements. One pen I made bends, so if you sit down and it's in your pocket, it won't break or hurt you. This is the nature of the things I do.

JD: One magazine predicted that what finance was to the '70s and marketing was to the '80s, design will be to the '90s. What do you think?

EA: Perhaps in Italy. In 1972, I curated an Italian design show at the Museum of Modern Art and have since followed that country closely. It was a poor country which made a commitment to quality and innovation and invention, rather than to low wages or inexpensive products.

JD: Is it working?

EA: For them, indeed. It's no secret that the Japanese have also observed it closely. That's probably why they're so far ahead of everyone else.

JD: How so?

EA: The Japanese are much more concerned with being great managers of information—information about developing new products—intelligent, valued-added products. They do not want their children to be highly-paid workers, nor even highly-paid bureaucrats—they want them to be highly-paid managers of information, almost like a banker manages financial capital. Those are the people who make the highest salaries.

JD: Accordingly, then, they'll have to rule the world.

EA: They're no longer concerned with things like quality control. Why should they worry about quality control when they have convinced the Americans to worry about it? When they could get the guys in Mexico to produce quality products with the same quality as they make them in Nagoya.

JD: What's your evidence of this?

EA: Plenty. I work for several different Japanese companies that are actively engaged in trying to construct products that will satisfy needs in the future. It's like they're making partial configurations of what the future may be.

Take a company like Sony. When they put a product on the market, it is considered dead the day it appears. At that minute, they start developing three alternative products. One of them, has a 10 to 15 percent improvement on price. Another has a fifty percent mechanical or manufacturing improvement. The third is a mutant. The financing of this new product is based on the income of the old one. In their bookkeeping system, they don't require the one on the market to pay for itself before they begin developing a new one.

JD: So how can America compete with that?

EA: It's simple: Americans should rekindle their love of becoming students. They should learn from their masters, whether at home or abroad, and they should study other peoples' minds and achievements. That's what the Japanese do from elementary school. Therein lies the secret; the rest is nonsense.

JD: What about this equation: when there is a downturn in the economy there is less emphasis on design. Is that true, and if so, how can it be refigured?

EA: You need new products whether the economy is in a downturn or in an upturn. There's no way a society based on creating products can suddenly believe that it no longer has to make products. America has committed itself to intermediation.

JD: Intermediation?

EA: Yes, buying and selling. It's the easy way. There's no responsibility, no risk, no long-term headaches. The only drawback to transferring the responsibility of making a product to somebody else, is that you are given a very small profit margin —buy at eight, sell at eight and a quarter.

JD: But clearly this country is comprised of more than just middlemen?

EA: When I was at the Museum of Modern Art, I presented five objects of high technology for the collection. All five were American technology but four were assembled in Europe. The Bang and Olafson record player was one of the choices and it exemplifies my point. The chips came from Texas Instruments and they cost about $15. They were assembled in Denmark, where it sold wholesale for about $290. By the time it got here, it was going for about $600. Fifteen dollars remained in Texas, $200 remained in Denmark.

The point is that all the parts were American but the labor was being given to an outside country, and that is of great concern. To me, he whom invents ways of providing labor should be given the Nobel Peace Prize. That's the answer to your question about what you do in a downturn: You make products. Labor is work. You can't base an economy on intermediation.

JD: Would you prefer a company run by a designer to a company run by an MBA?

EA: I think that the errors made by a designer would be far less catastrophic than the errors made by a bottom line man. Unless the corporation understands that it is in the business of inventing products that provide better solutions, there is no hope. And I assure you that very few corporations understand this. Even the enlightened ones. You need financial capital, yes, but you also have to have intellectual capital. This is the up-and-coming way of measuring success.

JD: Our last recession was fifteen years ago. Do you think there is any lesson to be learned from that in terms of the way products are made and manufactured today?

EA: You have a society that is in recession because, in part, it has changed its values. Today we value immediate gratification. There is no encouragement for industrialists in the United States to invest in product making because medium- and long-term investments are immediately punished by Wall Street. Companies have to make a profit and if they don't, the stock immediately falls, and when that happens, people try to take over the company. Nor is there encouragement in the tax system for new product development. You are much better off having a financial officer handling the corporation because you earn more that way.

JD: Do you think that a recession might frighten certain manufacturers to decide that some of their products at least need a face lift?

EA: The problem is not with American manufacturers. Like hunters wanting to survive in the jungle, they are pretty agile. But I find that the jungle has really restricted the possibilities of movement. With the current financial and tax system, there is no reason to take a risk. When you have a company rewarded for taking debt and not for risking a new product, what do you do? Probably, you buy another company instead of making anything new. Why explore for oil when you can find it on Wall Street?

JD: How do product designers then, make themselves more useful to the people who use their services?

EA: The designer is a powerless entity in the corporate organization. He is not involved in decision making, because decision makers don't feel that you can gain insight into a problem by asking a designer for an invention.

Let me give you a minor example. The story of the Sony Walkman is well known: Morita was told by everyone that nobody wants to go around with a silly little radio on his ears. But he was the owner of the company, so he did it, and he discovered an immense market. So now, Morita calls in the marketing people, and listens to their projections for products based on trends. He does that on one Friday, and the next Friday he calls in the designers and asks them to propose products. They're not supposed to talk numbers or statistics. They simply propose products, invent artifacts. Out of a hundred, maybe two are interesting. But they're asking designers to project tomorrow using existing technologies. This is the way of the future.

JD: Obsolescence is critical to the design profession; without it, you'd be out of a job. How does society balance the need for the new with the environmental concerns that it inevitably raises?

EA: You tax the product from the day it is born, so that its burial costs are paid for in advance. You don't allow the company to take all the profits and force the society to carry the cost of disposal. This means that there will be a reduction in the number of products consumers will be able to buy because they will cost more. And buyers will have to start making choices because there will be a certain restriction in a number of vaulable things, which, of course, is completely contrary to present thought. It's a poisonous notion. I will be invited to dinner by the presidents of the three auto manufacturers in Detroit and they'll serve me a meal, which will probably be my last one.

JD: How would you explain your profession to your five-year-old daughter, if you have one?

EA: I'd simply let the water run out of the faucet and tell her to drink. She would then look for a cup and I would ask her to make her own. Maybe she would pick up an empty shell of a grapefruit. Then she might ornament the shell with things that somehow represent the spirit dwelling inside the product. Hopefully that is an explanation and not rhetoric.

JD: And how would you explain it to your 75-year-old mother?

EA: This is a lost cause.

JD: If you were to teach design, what texts would be mandatory reading?

EA: *The Philosophy of the Future,* by Ernst Bloch. He was a communist philosopher, completely apostate according to the Communists, because he thought there was no way of acting ethically in the present without an image of the future as a guide. Second, *The Poetics of Space,* by Gaston Bachelard which is an exploration of the space which dwells in architecture. I would also ask them to listen to Russian poetry. They wouldn't understand the words, but they would hear the sounds and hopefully understand that sound is matter. They will thereby understand material in some abstract, but realistic way, and rhythm, cadence, proportion as well. Finally, *Philosophy of Method,* to study the way you organize and approach a problem so that it becomes manageable.

JD: What is most useful to a student of design today: a degree in philosophy, business, or Japanese?

EA: I really think a course in the making of idols—totem poles, saints, etc...Every culture makes idols in which it believes. They are the physical embodiment of that which is revered and worshipped. Essentially, it would be a course for shamans.

JD: What is your favorite ready-made object?

EA: The sewing needle, because I know how to make it better.

JD: Oh?

EA: You take the thread and you dip it into a certain plastic which becomes hard. You can then stitch with a hard tip of the thread.

JD: Thereby eliminating the needle?

EA: That's my reverse answer to the standard statement made by designers that it is an impossible product to improve. They haven't delved deeply enough into the root of what is needed.

JD: What's the most beautiful object you come in contact with every day?

EA: In New York, I live in a house with no furniture except for a bean bag chair. Every time I want to sit down, I have to decide the shape I want the seat to take, and then I get to make it. To me, what's beautiful is something I can somehow transform.

JD: What's the worst thing about being a designer?

EA: Not being the client. I think the designer should make products to meet his own expectations.

JD: What's the best thing?

EA: That you can make a model of a product you invent, in a solitary room, and you can see its scale, its texture, and imagine that it is alive. And perhaps, if it's not very technically or electronically endowed, you can fool yourself into thinking that it has been born.

PRODUCT

**Telephone/Facsimile
Concept**

DESIGNERS

**Greg Breiding
Spencer Murrell**

MANUFACTURER

Mitsubishi Electric

PHOTOGRAPHER

Steven Trank

PRODUCT
PR75 Compact Telephone
DESIGNER
O. Pena
MANUFACTURER
Philips

PRODUCT
Europorty Portable Telephone
DESIGNER
T. Overthun
MANUFACTURER
Philips

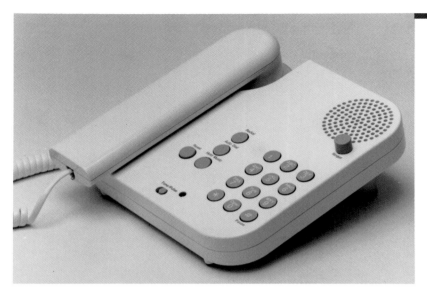

PRODUCT
Space-Tel Telephone
DESIGNER
**Morison S. Cousins—
Cousins Design, Inc.**
MANUFACTURER
**Atari Telephone (Warner
Communications)**
PHOTOGRAPHER
Cousins Design

PRODUCT
Aqua-Fone
DESIGNER
Mark Steiner
MANUFACTURER
**Proposed Product—
Steiner Design**
PHOTOGRAPHER
K. Kessler

PRODUCT

Dancall Logic Mobile Telephone

DESIGNER

IDEO Product Development and Cancall

MANUFACTURER

Dancall A/S, Denmark

PRODUCT

Vicom Set

DESIGNERS

Eric Chan, ECCO Design Inc.
Howard Citron, NYNEX

MANUFACTURER

NYNEX Corporation, Science and Technology Division

PRODUCT

Automobile Telephone

DESIGNER

GK Sekkei Incorporated

MANUFACTURER

Nippon Telegraph and Telephone

PHOTOGRAPHER

Masaaki Umeda

PRODUCT

Companion Baby Monitor

DESIGNERS

Roy Fischer, Randall Toltzman—Designology Inc.

MANUFACTURER

Cordogen Enterprises

PHOTOGRAPHER

Margaret Egan

PRODUCT

M^1 Stereo Speaker

DESIGNERS

**Ravi Sawhney
Lance Hussey
Cary Chow**

PHOTOGRAPHER

Lance Hussey

PRODUCT

Wavecatcher AM/FM Antenna

DESIGNER

Andy Vong

MANUFACTURER

Parsec of Delaware

PHOTOGRAPHERS

**Andy Johnson
Greg Savage**

PRODUCT
SBC 3208 Active Speaker Box
DESIGNER
R. Lewis
MANUFACTURER
Philips

PRODUCT
Speaker
DESIGNER
Hervé Houplain
MANUFACTURER
Lexon, France
PHOTOGRAPHER
Gail Molina

PRODUCT
800 Series Loudspeakers
DESIGNER
Kenneth Grange

18

PRODUCT

AM/FM(pi) Powered Stereo Antenna

DESIGNERS

**Luc Heiligenstein
Stephen Melamed
Francois Geneve**

MANUFACTURER

TERK Technologies Corporation

PHOTOGRAPHER

Staff

PRODUCT

fam **Powered Stereo Antenna**

DESIGNERS

**Francois Geneve
Stephen Melamed
Luc Heiligenstein**

MANUFACTURER

TERK Technologies Corporation

PHOTOGRAPHER

Staff

PRODUCT

Goldstar PCP 100

DESIGNERS

Roy Fischer, Randall Toltzman—Designology Inc.

MANUFACTURER

Goldstar

PHOTOGRAPHER

Margaret Egan

PRODUCT

Access Control

DESIGNER

Ramon Benedito

MANUFACTURER

Fermax Electronics S.A.E.

PHOTOGRAPHER

S.F. Sanchez Peris

20

PRODUCT
Pocket Commander
DESIGNER
**Toru Irie, Fujitsu
Industrial Design Section**
MANUFACTURER
Fujitsu Limited

PRODUCT

20-inch Stereo Television

DESIGNERS

Tom Renk—Senior Industrial Designer Dennis Erber—Manager, Table Model & Portable Television Lou Lenzi—Manager, Industrial Design

MANUFACTURER

Thomson Consumer Electronics

PHOTOGRAPHER

Tom Wedell

PRODUCT

Prophecy TV

DESIGNERS

A. Gratton & R. Heynen

MANUFACTURER

Philips

PRODUCT

25-inch Direct View Television

DESIGNERS

Robert Huber—Senior Industrial Designer Denis Erber—Manager, Table Model & Portable Television Lou Lenzi—Manager, Industrial Design

MANUFACTURER

Thomson Consumer Electronics

PHOTOGRAPHER

Tom Wedell

PRODUCT

13-inch Television

DESIGNERS

**Tom Renk—Senior
Industrial Designer
Dennis Erber—Manager,
Table Model & Portable
Television
Lou Lenzi—Manager,
Industrial Design**

MANUFACTURER

**Thomson Consumer
Electronics**

PHOTOGRAPHER

Format, Inc.

PRODUCT

Loewe Art Vision 2

DESIGNER

**Neumeister Design,
Munich**

MANUFACTURER

Loewe Opta GmbH

PRODUCT
Your TV
DESIGNERS
D. Thackray & D. Hartman
MANUFACTURER
Philips

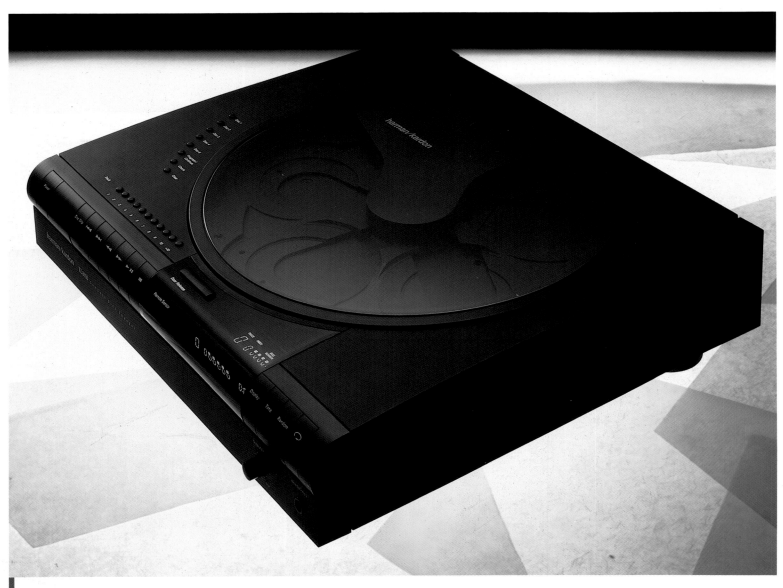

PRODUCT

TL 8600 CD Carousel

DESIGNERS

Dan Ashcraft
Scott Shimatsu

MANUFACTURER

Harman Kardon

PHOTOGRAPHER

Henry Blackham

PRODUCT

GV2030X

DESIGNERS

Roy Fischer, Randall Toltzman—Designology Inc.

MANUFACTURER

Go-Video Inc.

PHOTOGRAPHER

Designology—David Kern

PRODUCT
YST-DC11 Micro Table-top Audio System
DESIGNER
GK Incorporated
MANUFACTURER
Yamaha Corporation
PHOTOGRAPHER
Masaaki Umeda

PRODUCT
Solo AM/FM Radio
DESIGNERS
**Gordon Randall Perry
Thomas Van Dyk**
MANUFACTURER
Wise USA
PHOTOGRAPHER
Gordon Randall Perry

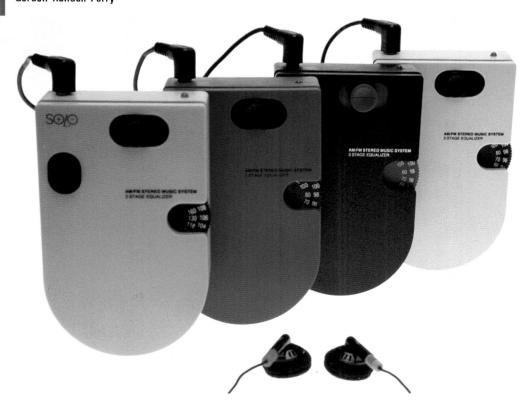

PRODUCT
DC 720 Range
DESIGNER
D. Hautbout
MANUFACTURER
Philips

PRODUCT

**Airtronics Infinity Radio
Controller**

DESIGNERS

**Jim Grove—Vice President
John Cook, Fernando Pardo
—Senior Designers
Tim Renaud, Bob Renaud,
Barbara Renaud-Airtronics
Design**

PHOTOGRAPHER

John Cook

PRODUCT

**RCA 25 inch Stereo
Monitor/Receiver**

DESIGNER

Robert Huber

MANUFACTURER

**Thomson Consumer
Electronics**

PRODUCT

PCL 320 Notebook PC

DESIGNERS

**G. Proctor
W. Thijssen**

MANUFACTURER

Philips

PRODUCT
TONWS 2 Model UX
DESIGNERS
**Atsuo Takanezawa
Kohichi Kawano, Fujitsu
Industrial Design**
MANUFACTURER
Fujitsu Limited

PRODUCT
Retractable Wall Cord
DESIGNERS
Mark Steiner, Ben Gorbaty
MANUFACTURER
Proposed Product
PHOTOGRAPHER
M. Steiner

PRODUCT

Precision Cursor

DESIGNERS

**IDEO Product
Development:
Marc Tanner—Senior
Designer
Charles Ash/Geoff Gray—
Mechanical Engineering
Paul South/Roger
Penn/Jorge Davies—
Modelmaking Development**

MANUFACTURER

TDS Numonics

PRODUCT

Air Purifier

DESIGNERS

Frank R. Wilgus, Don Staufenberg, Andreas Roessner, Inars Jurjans, Frank A. Wilgus, Deane W. Richardson—Fitch RichardsonSmith

MANUFACTURER

Duskin Co., Ltd.—Osaka, Japan

PRODUCT

Sapphire Midi Pedestal Fan

DESIGNER

Arvind B. Joshi

MANUFACTURER

Rallifan, Bombay, India

PHOTOGRAPHER

Arvind B. Joshi

PRODUCT

Sunbeam 900 Air Purifier & Ionizer

DESIGNERS

**Stephen Melamed
Luc Heiligenstein
Francois Geneve
Richard Riback**

MANUFACTURER

**Sunbeam—Home Comfort Division
Chicago, Illinois**

PHOTOGRAPHER

Bob Sacco

PRODUCT

Emerson Quiet Kool Dehumidifier

DESIGNER

Henry Dreyfuss Associates

MANUFACTURER

Emerson Quiet Kool

PHOTOGRAPHER

Henry Dreyfuss Associates (in-house)

PRODUCT

"Equator" Heater/ Humidifier

DESIGNER

Roy Fischer—Designology Inc.

MANUFACTURER

Steman & Co.

PHOTOGRAPHER

Margaret Egan

PRODUCT
**Eurorange Vacuum
Cleaner**
DESIGNER
A. Jack
MANUFACTURER
Philips

PRODUCT
E-Range Hairdryers
DESIGNER
S. Wilkinson
MANUFACTURER
Philips

PRODUCT

**ST400, ST420, ST450
Electric Steam Irons**

DESIGNER

**Kenneth Grange,
Pentagram**

MANUFACTURER

Kenwood Limited (U.K.)

PHOTOGRAPHER

Nick Turner

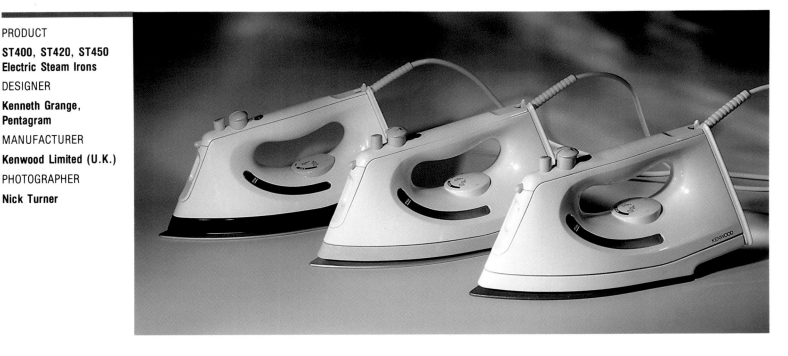

PRODUCT

Rallimix (Food Processor)

DESIGNER

Arvind B. Joshi

MANUFACTURER

Rallis India Ltd., Bombay

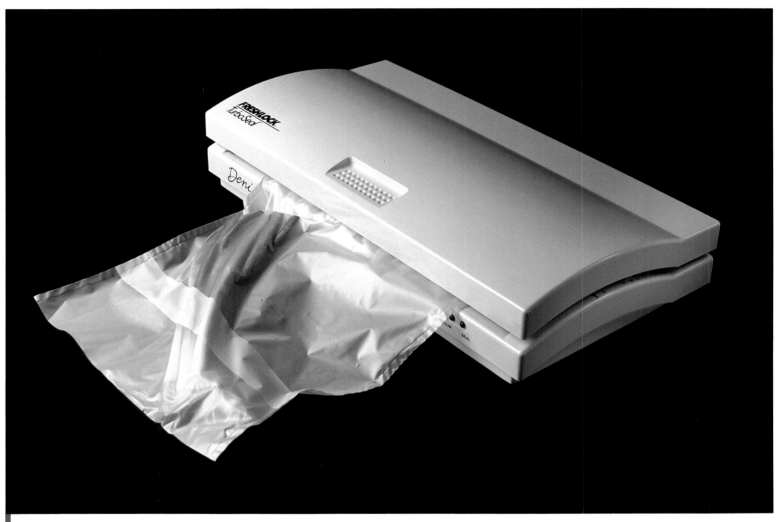

PRODUCT

Vacuum Sealer

DESIGNERS

Gregg Davis
Tim Friar
Diana Juratovac
John Koenig

MANUFACTURER

Deni Keystone

PHOTOGRAPHER

Larry Friar

PRODUCT

Rowenta TP-100 Sensor
Electronic Toaster

DESIGNER

Rowenta GmbH

MANUFACTURER

Rowenta GmbH

PHOTOGRAPHER

Ken Skalski

PRODUCT

UKettle

DESIGNERS

**Michael Jaeb, Gavin
Jewel, Scott Stropkay,
Dave Privatera—Polymer
Solutions**

MANUFACTURER

Great British Kettles, Ltd.

PHOTOGRAPHER

**Mark A. Steele, Fitch
Richardsonsmith**

PRODUCT

**''Non Plus Ultra''
Kitchen's Cooking
Equipment**

DESIGNER

Strato

PRODUCT
Gaggenau CK 394
DESIGNER
Gaggenau Design Team
MANUFACTURER
Gaggenau Werke
PHOTOGRAPHER
Claus A. Froh

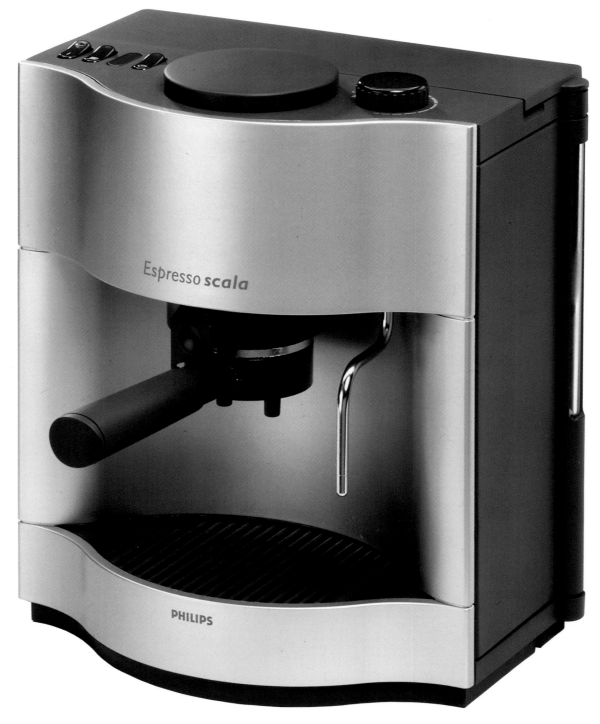

PRODUCT
Espresso Scala
DESIGNER
L. Beeren
MANUFACTURER
Philips

PRODUCT

**Rowenta FK-29
Programmable
Coffeemaker**

DESIGNER

Rowenta GmbH

MANUFACTURER

Rowenta GmbH

PHOTOGRAPHER

Ken Skalski

PRODUCT
Wings
DESIGNER
Hervé Houplain
MANUFACTURER
Lexon, France
PHOTOGRAPHER
Gail Molina

PRODUCT

**Roland US Activ-NF-25
Near Field Studio Monitors**

DESIGNERS

**Fernando Pardo
James Grove
Graphics, Kyle Paula**

MANUFACTURER

LM Acoustics

PHOTOGRAPHER

Greg Savage

PRODUCT
Easy Line Range
DESIGNER
L. Pepall
MANUFACTURER
Philips

PRODUCT
Autopilot—the Benmar 2000
DESIGNER
Vladymir Rogov
MANUFACTURER
Benmar Marine Electronics
PHOTOGRAPHER
Kevin Halley

PRODUCT
'vik-t*e*r stacking chair
DESIGNER
Dakota Jackson
MANUFACTURER
Dakota Jackson, Inc.
PHOTOGRAPHER
John Bessler

PRODUCT
Perry Chair
DESIGNER
Charles O. Perry
MANUFACTURER
Krueger International
PHOTOGRAPHER
Krueger International
PHOTOGRAPHER
David Wallace, Image Studios

PRODUCT
Leopold Chair
DESIGNER
James Geier and Automatic Inc.
MANUFACTURER
Automatic Inc.
PHOTOGRAPHER
Automatic Inc.

PRODUCT
Ears Barstool
DESIGNER
Ries Niemi
MANUFACTURER
Ries Niemi
PHOTOGRAPHER
Ries Niemi

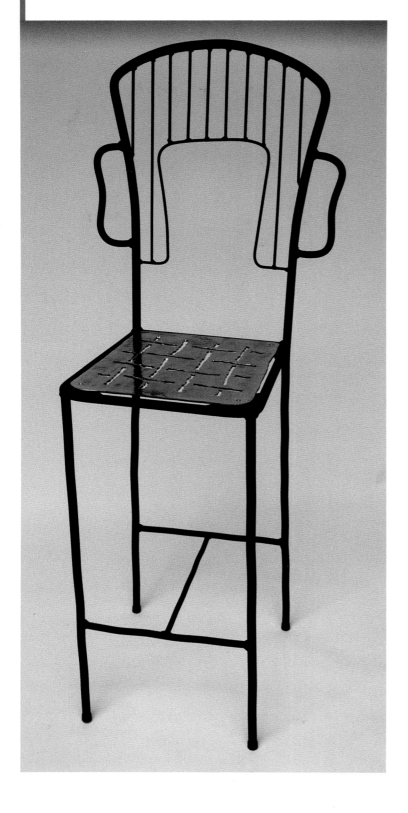

PRODUCT
Alice—Design 1991
DESIGNER
Claudio Nardi
MANUFACTURER
Noto / Zeus
PHOTOGRAPHER
Bitetto—Chimenti

PRODUCT
Troika
DESIGNER
Eduard Samsó
MANUFACTURER
Carlos Jane Camacho

PRODUCT
Bra Chair
DESIGNER
Zev Vaughn
MANUFACTURER
Public Domain
PHOTOGRAPHER
Zev Vaughn

PRODUCT
Wedges Chair
DESIGNER
David Gray
MANUFACTURER
Bruce Gray/Gray Design
PHOTOGRAPHER
Bruce Gray

PRODUCT
''Reach Chair''
DESIGNER
**Ross Anderson, Anderson/
Schwartz Architects**
MANUFACTURER
Greg Curry
PHOTOGRAPHER
Steve Moore

PRODUCT
Porto
DESIGNER
Oscar Tusquets
MANUFACTURER
Carlos Jane Camacho

PRODUCT

Sussex Chair

DESIGNERS

Brian Kane, Kane Design Studio

MANUFACTURER

Bernhardt Furniture Co.

PHOTOGRAPHER

Burns & Associates

PRODUCT

The Gehry Collection

DESIGNER

Frank Gehry

MANUFACTURER

The Knoll Group

PHOTOGRAPHER

Jay Ahrend

PRODUCT
**Maple and Walnut Sap
Molded Chair**
DESIGNER
Skip Abelson
MANUFACTURER
Skip Abelson

50

PRODUCT
Alpha Arm Chair
DESIGNER
**James Geier and
Automatic Inc.**
MANUFACTURER
Automatic Inc.
PHOTOGRAPHER
Automatic Inc.

PRODUCT
Kite—Kite/R
DESIGNER
Anna Anselmi
MANUFACTURER
**Bieffe Di B. Ferrarese
S.P.A.**

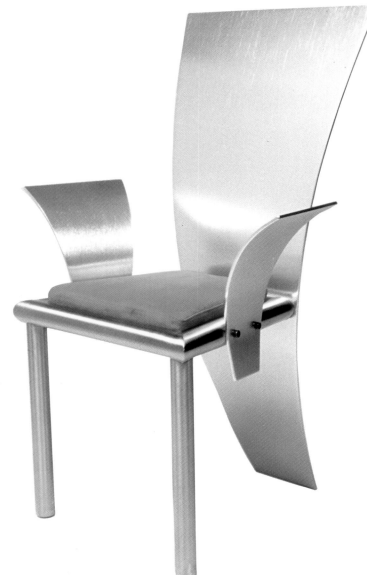

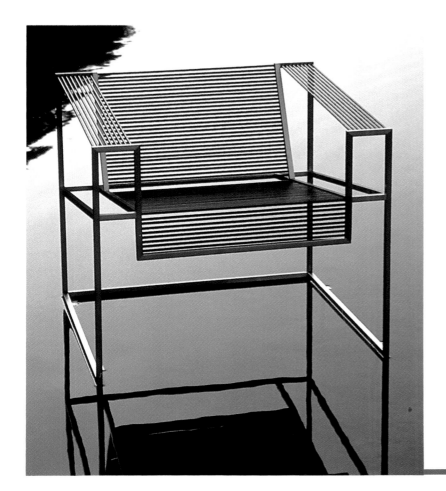

PRODUCT
Willow
DESIGNER
Mitchell Pickard
MANUFACTURER
Brueton Industries

PRODUCT
"Supernova 1991 A"
DESIGNER
Shozo Toyohisa
MANUFACTURER
Kit Art Co., Ltd. and Super Lattice
PHOTOGRAPHER
Nobuo Tanaka

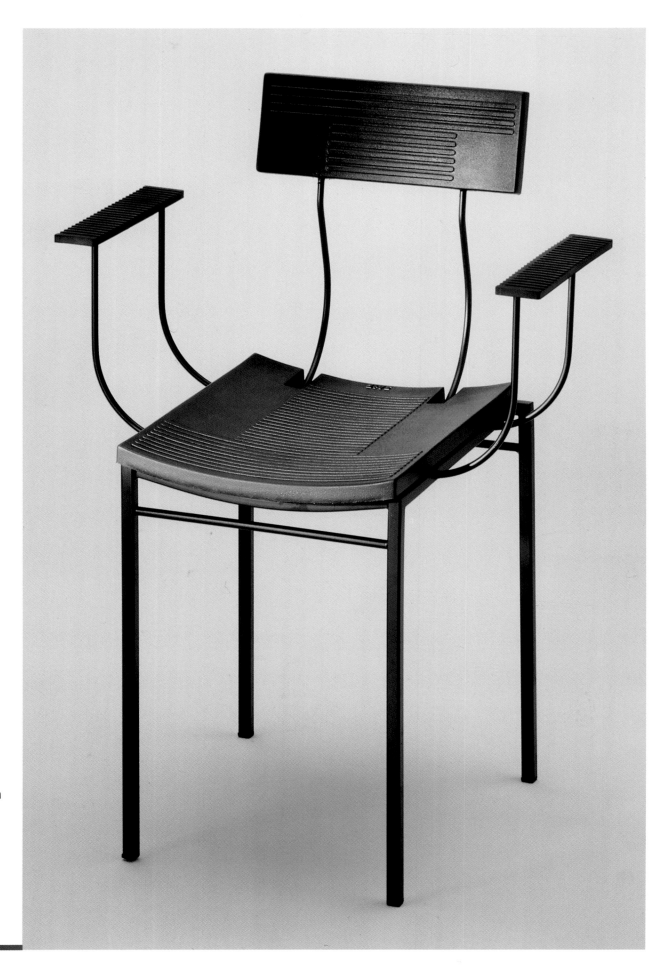

PRODUCT
Glasnost Poltrona—Design 1991
DESIGNER
Maurizio Peregalli
MANUFACTURER
Noto / Zeus
PHOTOGRAPHER
Bitetto—Chimenti

PRODUCT
Ram Chair
DESIGNERS
Monique Savarese
Sergio Savarese
MANUFACTURER
Dialogica
PHOTOGRAPHER
Nancy Hill

PRODUCT
**Made In America Indoor/
Outdoor Chair**
DESIGNER
**Kenny Farrell, O.P.M.
Design**
MANUFACTURER
Kenny Farrell
PHOTOGRAPHER
Don Fukuda

PRODUCT
Much Obliged Rocker
DESIGNER
Philip Miller
MANUFACTURER
Philip Miller

PRODUCT
Click Clack Folding Chair
DESIGNER
**Kenny Farrell, O.P.M.
Design**
MANUFACTURER
Kenny Farrell
PHOTOGRAPHER
Kenny Farrell

PRODUCT
HYPNOS-Relaxation Chair
DESIGNER
GK Incorporated
MANUFACTURER
Lofty Co., LTD
PHOTOGRAPHER
Takato Kaburagi

PRODUCT
Perry Glass Chair
DESIGNER
Gordon Randall Perry
MANUFACTURER
Perry Design Inc.
PHOTOGRAPHER
Gordon Randall Perry

PRODUCT
Sol, Theres, Paloma, Isabel/ Family of Four Side Chairs
DESIGNER
Kenny Farrell, O.P.M. Design
MANUFACTURER
Kenny Farrell
PHOTOGRAPHER
Kenny Farrell

PRODUCT

**Paramus Seating
Collection**

DESIGNER

**Brian Kane, Kane Design
Studio**

MANUFACTURER

Bernhardt Furniture Co.

PHOTOGRAPHER

Burns & Associates

PRODUCT

Morristown Seating Collection

DESIGNER

Brian Kane, Kane Design Studio

MANUFACTURER

Bernhardt Furniture Co.

PHOTOGRAPHER

Burns & Associates

PRODUCT
Apparition Sofa
DESIGNER
John Hutton
MANUFACTURER
Donghia Furniture

PRODUCT
Tribute Settee
DESIGNERS
Paul Ruine
Cheryl L. Ruine
MANUFACTURER
Ruine Design Associates
PHOTOGRAPHER
John Montana

PRODUCT
Rope Sofa and Chair
DESIGNER
Stanley Jay Friedman
MANUFACTURER
Brueton Industries
PHOTOGRAPHER
Peter Paige

PRODUCT
Cody Club Chair
DESIGNER
**James Geier and
Automatic Inc.**
MANUFACTURER
Automatic Inc.
PHOTOGRAPHER
Automatic Inc.

PRODUCT
Artu—armchair
DESIGNER
Isao Hosoe
MANUFACTURER
Cassina spa, Italy

PRODUCT
Allora
DESIGNER
Victor I. Dziekiewicz
MANUFACTURER
Brueton Industries

PRODUCT

Oom Loose Seat Lounge Chair

DESIGNERS

Monique Savarese
Sergio Savarese

MANUFACTURER

Dialogica

PHOTOGRAPHER

Nancy Hill

PRODUCT
DSN Sofa
DESIGNER
David Shaw Nicholls
MANUFACTURER
Palazzetti

PRODUCT
Oscar Sofa
DESIGNERS
**Monique Savarese
Sergio Savarese**
MANUFACTURER
Dialogica
PHOTOGRAPHER
Nancy Hill

PRODUCT
Sofa For Museum Hall
DESIGNER
GK Sekkei Incorporated
MANUFACTURER
**Hiroshima City Museum of
Contemporary Art**
PHOTOGRAPHER
Nacasa & Partners

PRODUCT
Griffon Chaise
DESIGNERS
Paul Ruine
Cheryl L. Ruine
MANUFACTURER
Ruine Design Associates
PHOTOGRAPHER
John Montana

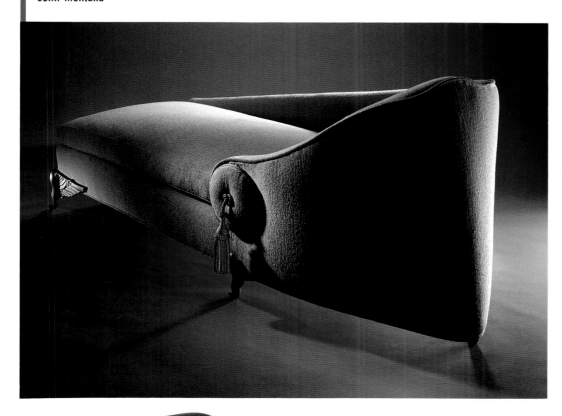

PRODUCT
Chaise Lounge
DESIGNER
Mats Theselius
MANUFACTURER
Källemo AB, Sweden
PHOTOGRAPHER
Curt Ekblom

PRODUCT
My Darling Bed
DESIGNERS
**Monique Savarese
Sergio Savarese**
MANUFACTURER
Dialogica
PHOTOGRAPHER
Nancy Hill

PRODUCT
"Medicine Chest"
DESIGNER
Lisa Krivacka
MANUFACTURER
Lisa Krivacka
PHOTOGRAPHER
Adam Reich

PRODUCT
"Toy Chest"
DESIGNER
Lisa Krivacka
MANUFACTURER
Lisa Krivacka
PHOTOGRAPHER
Adam Reich

70

PRODUCT

Forpointe Love Seat

DESIGNER

**James Geier and
Automatic Inc.**

MANUFACTURER

Automatic Inc.

PHOTOGRAPHER

Automatic Inc.

PRODUCT

B 320 Public Seating Line

DESIGNER

ECCO Design Inc., Eric Chan

MANUFACTURER

RPI Inc., Marlette, MI

PRODUCT

Promenade Modular Seating System

DESIGNER

Nick Balderi

MANUFACTURER

Krueger International

PHOTOGRAPHER

Steve Ryan, Ryan's Commercial Photography

72

PRODUCT
Maple Slanted Side Table
DESIGNERS
Skip Abelson
MANUFACTURER
Skip Abelson

PRODUCT
"S.F." Table
DESIGNER
Allen Miesner
MANUFACTURER
Miesner Design

PRODUCT
Vortice Coffee Table
DESIGNER
Oscar Tusquets Blanca
MANUFACTURER
Carlos Jane Camacho

PRODUCT
Nido Tables
DESIGNER
Giovanni Levanti
MANUFACTURER
Cassina S.p.A.

PRODUCT
Ying Yang Table
DESIGNER
Al Glass
MANUFACTURER
Modulus
PHOTOGRAPHER
David Lyles

PRODUCT
Atlantis Table
DESIGNER
Bill Becker
MANUFACTURER
BDI
PHOTOGRAPHER
Michael Latil

PRODUCT
Yucca Table
DESIGNER
Anna Anselmi
MANUFACTURER
**Bieffe Di B. Ferrarese
S.P.A.**

76
PRODUCT
Oak Series #3
DESIGNER
Michael Clapper
MANUFACTURER
Michael Clapper Design
PHOTOGRAPHER
Emile Ghinger

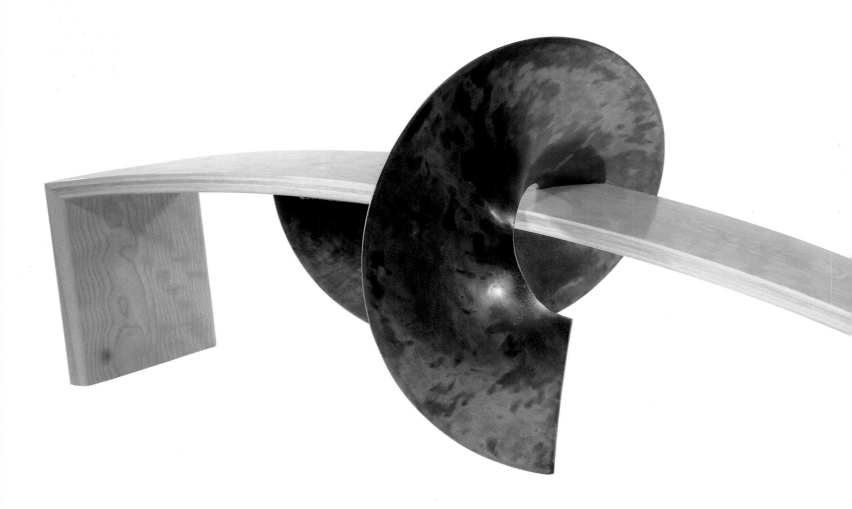

PRODUCT
Lioness Table
DESIGNER
Clodagh
MANUFACTURER
Clodagh Design International
PHOTOGRAPHER
Vlada Radojcic

PRODUCT
Wave Console Table
DESIGNER
Clodagh
MANUFACTURER
Clodagh Design International
PHOTOGRAPHER
Oberto Gili

PRODUCT
Curved Back Table #3
DESIGNER
Michael Clapper
MANUFACTURER
Michael Clapper Design
PHOTOGRAPHER
Paul Raynor

PRODUCT
''Dining Room Table''
DESIGNER
Lisa Krivacka
MANUFACTURER
Lisa Krivacka
PHOTOGRAPHER
Adam Reich

PRODUCT

**"Bio-Tables II"—
Playoffice System**

DESIGNERS

**Isao Hosoe in collaboration
with Masaya Hashimoto,
Ann Marinelli, Alessio
Pozzoli, Sam Ribet—Isao
Hosoe Design, Italy**

MANUFACTURER

Itoki Co., Ltd., Japan

PRODUCT
Hall Table
DESIGNER
Michael Clapper
MANUFACTURER
Michael Clapper Design
PHOTOGRAPHER
Page Steinhardt

PRODUCT
''Late Winter'' wall-mounted hall table
DESIGNER
Michael Clapper
MANUFACTURER
Michael Clapper Design
PHOTOGRAPHER
Michael Clapper

PRODUCT
"Flat & Floral"
DESIGNER
Allen Miesner
MANUFACTURER
Miesner Design

PRODUCT
"Lines"
DESIGNER
Shozo Toyohisa
MANUFACTURER
**Kilt Art Co., Ltd. and
Super Lattice**
PHOTOGRAPHER
Masayuki Okabe

PRODUCT
Double Gate Leg Table
DESIGNER
Dale Broholm
MANUFACTURER
Dale Broholm
PHOTOGRAPHER
Andrew Dean Powell

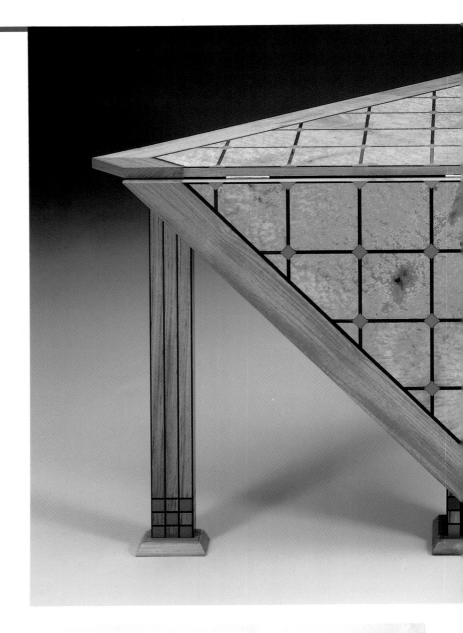

PRODUCT
''I'm a Table''
DESIGNERS
Ross Anderson and M.J. Sagan, Anderson/ Schwartz Architects
MANUFACTURER
Solo Metal Works, Ltd. and Steve Truslow
PHOTOGRAPHER
Steve Moore

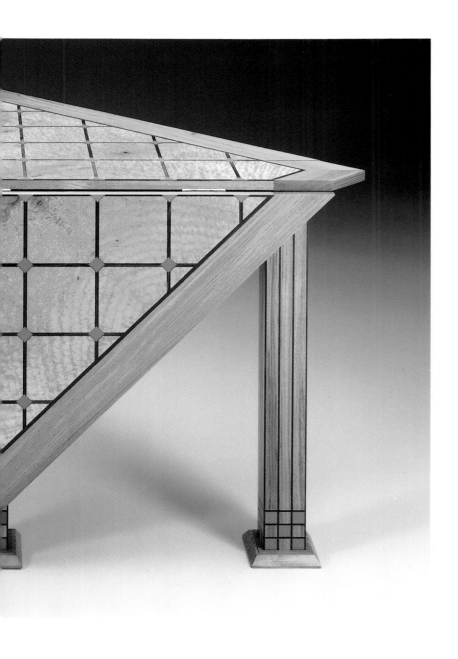

PRODUCT
Anasazi Cabinet
DESIGNER
Michael Clapper
MANUFACTURER
Michael Clapper Design
PHOTOGRAPHER
David Mohney

PRODUCT

Chest of Drawers

DESIGNER

**Tim Wells—The Pressure
Group**

MANUFACTURER

Tim Wells Furniture

PHOTOGRAPHER

David Mohney

PRODUCT

''Brothel Cabinet''

DESIGNER

**Richard Snyder
Available through Art et
Industrie**

PRODUCT

"Girl in a Blue Bottle".

DESIGNER

**Richard Snyder
Available through Art et
Industrie**

PRODUCT
Cabinet
DESIGNER
Fernd Van Engelen
MANUFACTURER
Section Five Design Ltd.
PHOTOGRAPHER
Fernd Van Engelen

PRODUCT
''The Dancing Bear Cabinet''
DESIGNER
Richard Snyder
Available through Art et
Industrie

PRODUCT

Stormo bookcase

DESIGNER

Isao Hosoe—Isao Hosoe Design, Italy

MANUFACTURER

Tonelli, srl, Italy

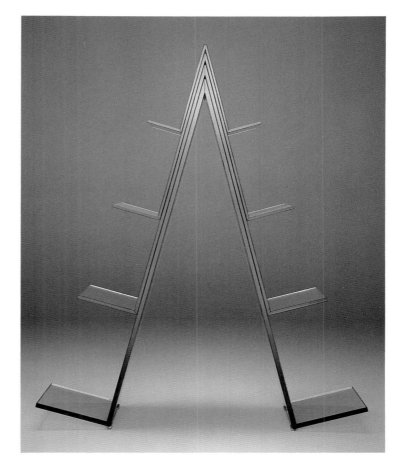

PRODUCT

"A" Frame Unit

DESIGNER

James Geier and 555 Design Fabrication Management

MANUFACTURER

555 Design Fabrication Management

PHOTOGRAPHER

555 Design Fabrication Management

PRODUCT
CDScape
DESIGNER
Al Glass
MANUFACTURER
BDI
PHOTOGRAPHER
Michael Latil

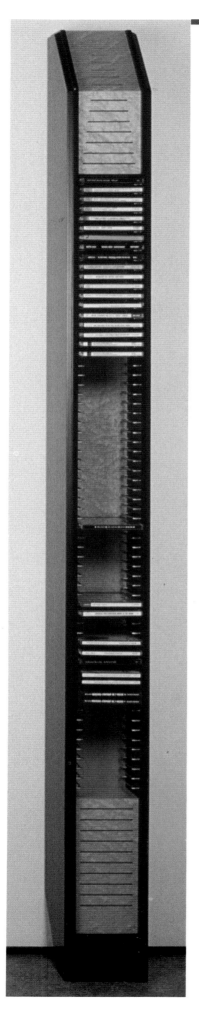

PRODUCT
''Lumidisc''
DESIGNER
Maison DUPIN SA—Pascal Luthi
MANUFACTURER
EBENISTERIE LUTHI SA

PRODUCT
Ecology
DESIGNER
Anna Anselmi
MANUFACTURER
Bieffe Di B. Ferrarese S.P.A.

PRODUCT

Floor Mirror—Wood

DESIGNER

James Geier and 555 Design Fabrication Management

MANUFACTURER

555 Design Fabrication Management

PHOTOGRAPHER

555 Design Fabrication Management

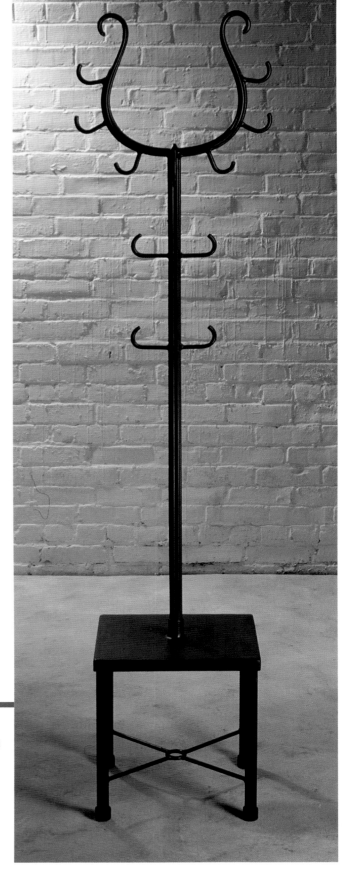

PRODUCT

''Coat Stand for Thor's House''

DESIGNER

Peter Diepenbrock

MANUFACTURER

Peter Diepenbrock

PHOTOGRAPHY

James Beards Photography

PRODUCT
Fireplace Screen
DESIGNER
Ries Niemi
MANUFACTURER
Ries Niemi
PHOTOGRAPHER
Ries Niemi

PRODUCT
Florian Table Lamp
DESIGNERS
Robert Gaul
Michele Michael
MANUFACTURER
Robert Gaul/Michele
Michael
PHOTOGRAPHER
Michael Grand

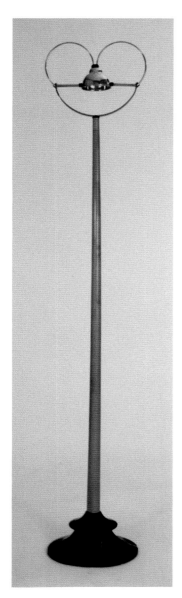

PRODUCT
Palais 1BL
DESIGNER
Matteo Thun
MANUFACTURER
Woka Lamps, Vienna

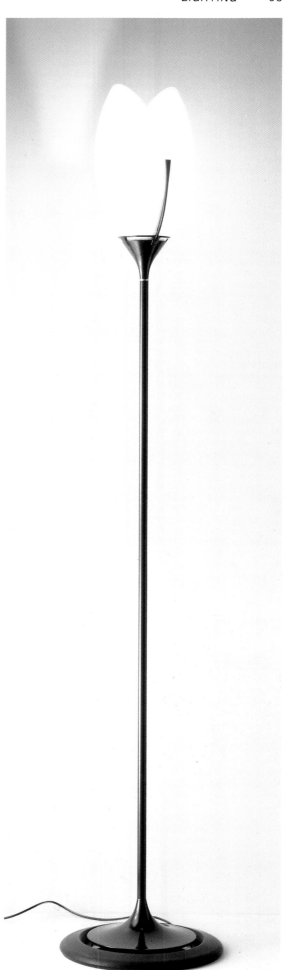

PRODUCT
Corolle
DESIGNER
Ezio Didone
MANUFACTURER
Flos

PRODUCT
Pao
DESIGNER
Matteo Thun
MANUFACTURER
Flos

PRODUCT
**"PYLON" Floor Lamp
with Adjustable Shelf**
DESIGNER
David Baird, Architect
MANUFACTURER
Ziggurat
PHOTOGRAPHER
Alan Linn

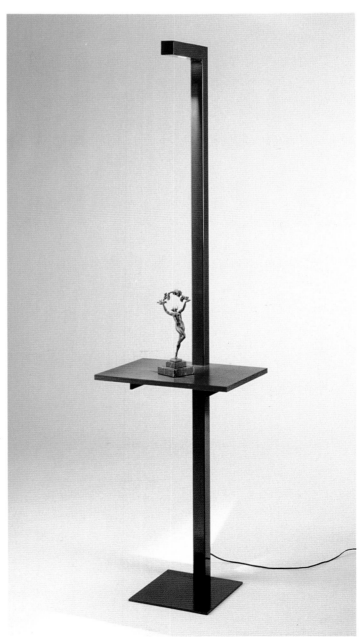

PRODUCT
"JESTOR" Floor Lamp
DESIGNER
David Baird, Architect
MANUFACTURER
Ziggurat
PHOTOGRAPHER
Alan Linn

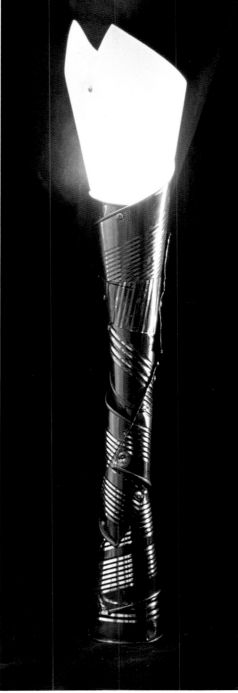

PRODUCT
Orpheus Lamp
DESIGNER
Lisa Krohn
MANUFACTURER
Krohn Design

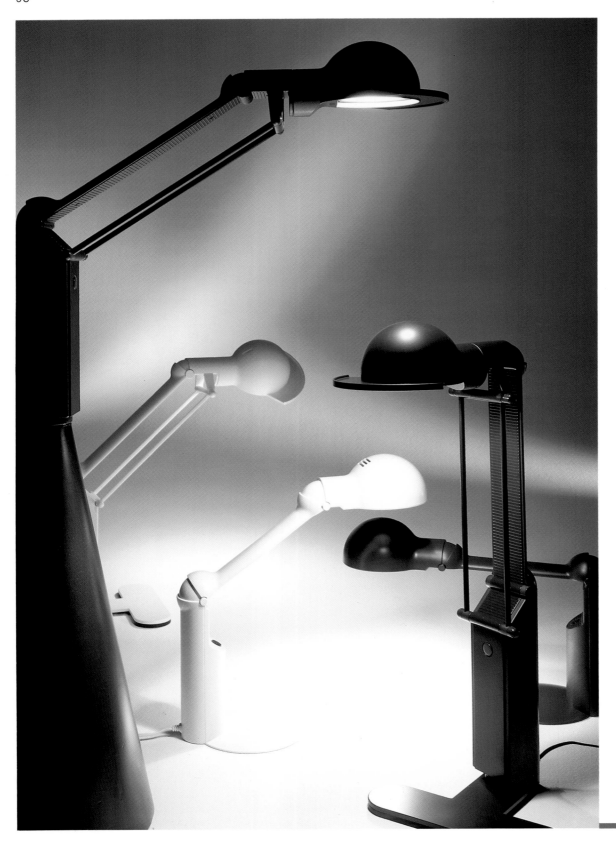

PRODUCT
Bio-Light
DESIGNER
Masayuki Kurokawa
MANUFACTURER
Paris Miki Incorporated
PHOTOGRAPHER
Akira Shimizu

PRODUCT
Nestore Floor Lamp
DESIGNER
Carlo Forcolini
MANUFACTURER
Artemide

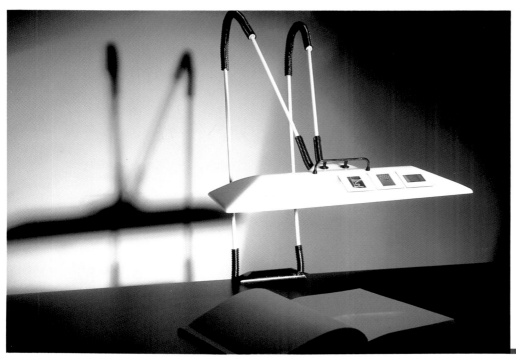

PRODUCT
**Slide Viewing Lamp
(Prototype)**
DESIGNER
Peter Skillman
PHOTOGRAPHER
Geoffrey Nelson

PRODUCT
BAP Light System
DESIGNERS
Alberto Meda, Paolo Rizzatto
MANUFACTURER
Luce Plan

PRODUCT
Squeeze Lamps: Freestanding, Suspended, Micro-suspended and Wall-mounted
DESIGNERS
Christian Dufay and Lisa Krohn
MANUFACTURER
George Kovacs Lighting Inc.
PHOTOGRAPHERS
Lisa Krohn, Christian Dufay, Tucker Viemeister

PRODUCT
Warrior Lamp
DESIGNER
Emanuele Ricci
MANUFACTURER
**Artemide ''Sidecar''
Collection**

PRODUCT
Aura Vetro
DESIGNERS
**Perry King
Santiago Miranda**
MANUFACTURER
Flos

PRODUCT
Dominique (Wall or Ceiling Mounted Fixture)
DESIGNER
Kevin L. Willmorth
MANUFACTURER
Winona Lighting
PHOTOGRAPHER
Kevin L. Willmorth

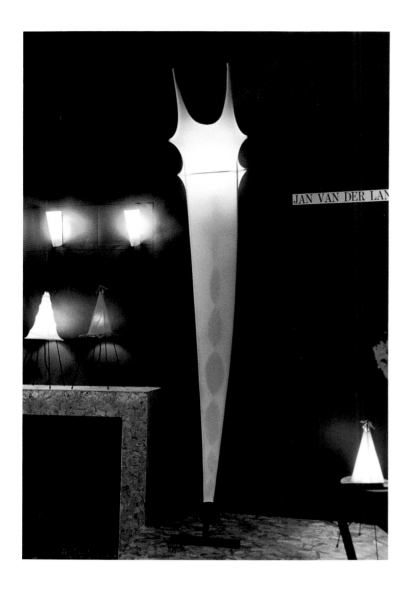

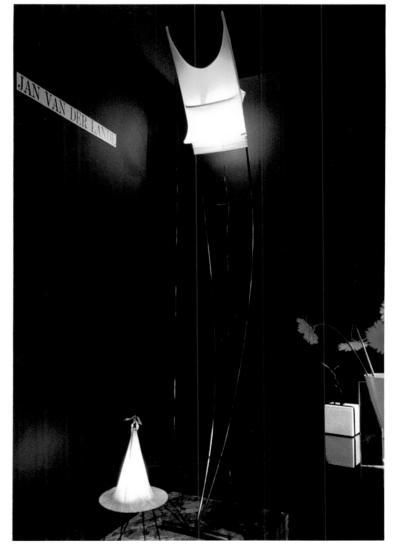

PRODUCT
Arc Lamps
DESIGNER
Lisa Krohn
MANUFACTURER
Krohn Design
PHOTOGRAPHER
Christian Dufay

PRODUCT
Madonie & Cefalu Table Lamps
DESIGNER
Martha Davis
MANUFACTURER
Able Industrial
PHOTOGRAPHER
Able

PRODUCT
Gelato Table Lamp
DESIGNER
Ron Rezek
MANUFACTURER
Ron Rezek
PHOTOGRAPHER
Allison Duke

PRODUCT
Miss Sissi
DESIGNER
Philippe Starck
MANUFACTURER
Flos

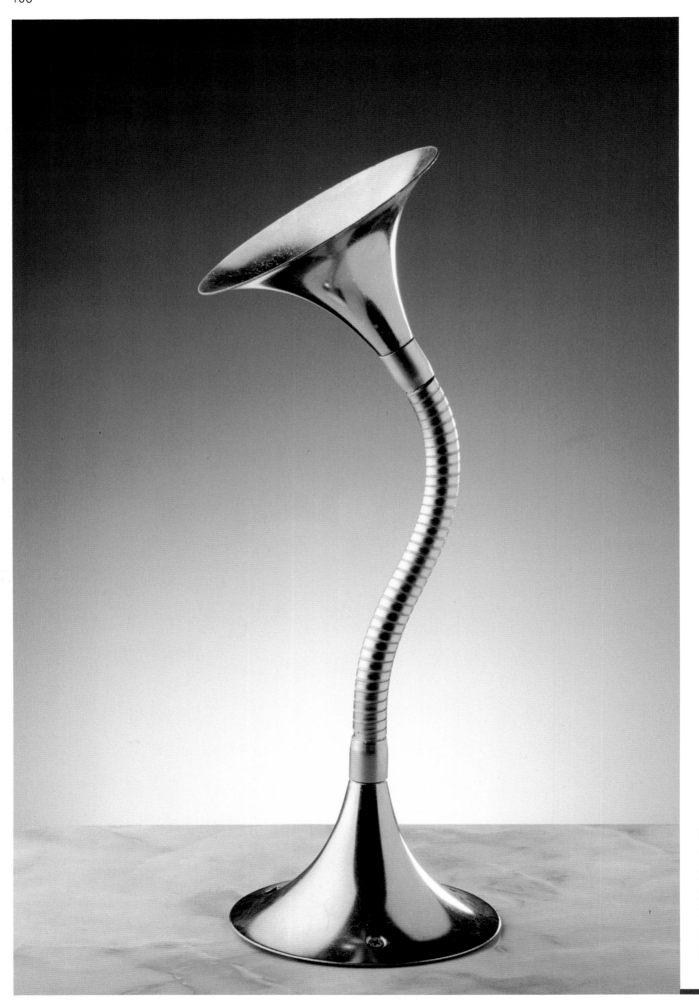

PRODUCT
"Metals Lamp"
DESIGNER
Davide Mercatali
MANUFACTURER
Metals
PHOTOGRAPHER
Marco Pirovallo

PRODUCT
Concord Chandelier
DESIGNER
Kevin L. Willmorth
MANUFACTURER
Winona Lighting
PHOTOGRAPHER
Kevin L. Willmorth

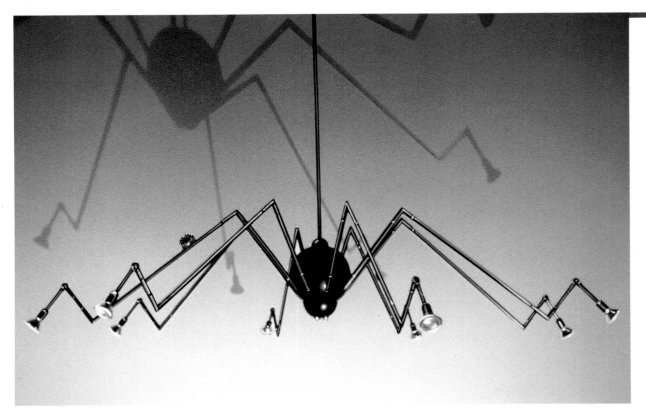

PRODUCT
Mimi
DESIGNER
Walter Schmoegner
MANUFACTURER
Woka Lamps, Vienna

PRODUCT
Kalea Lamp
DESIGNER
Vico Magistretti
MANUFACTURER
Artemide

PRODUCT
Velica
DESIGNERS
**Luciano Pagani
Angelo Perversi**
MANUFACTURER
Flos

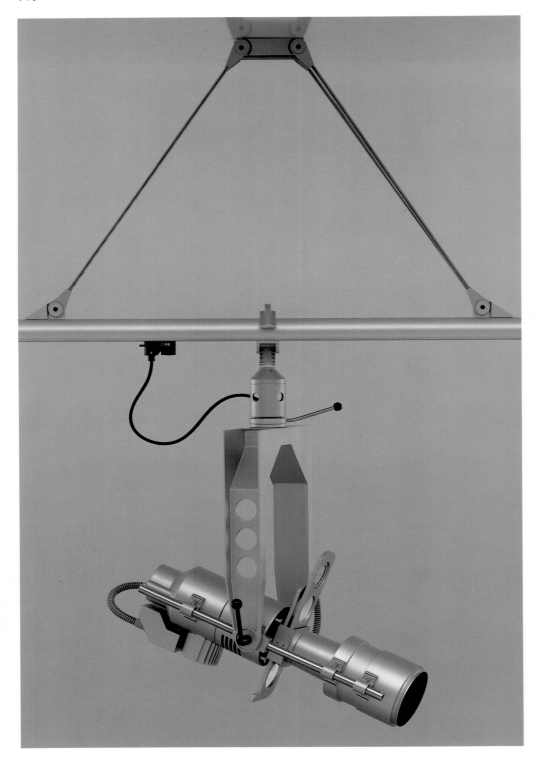

PRODUCT

Emanon Projector

DESIGNER

**Roy Fleetwood, Great
Britain**

MANUFACTURER

ERCO Leuchten GmbH

PHOTOGRAPHER

Hans Hansen

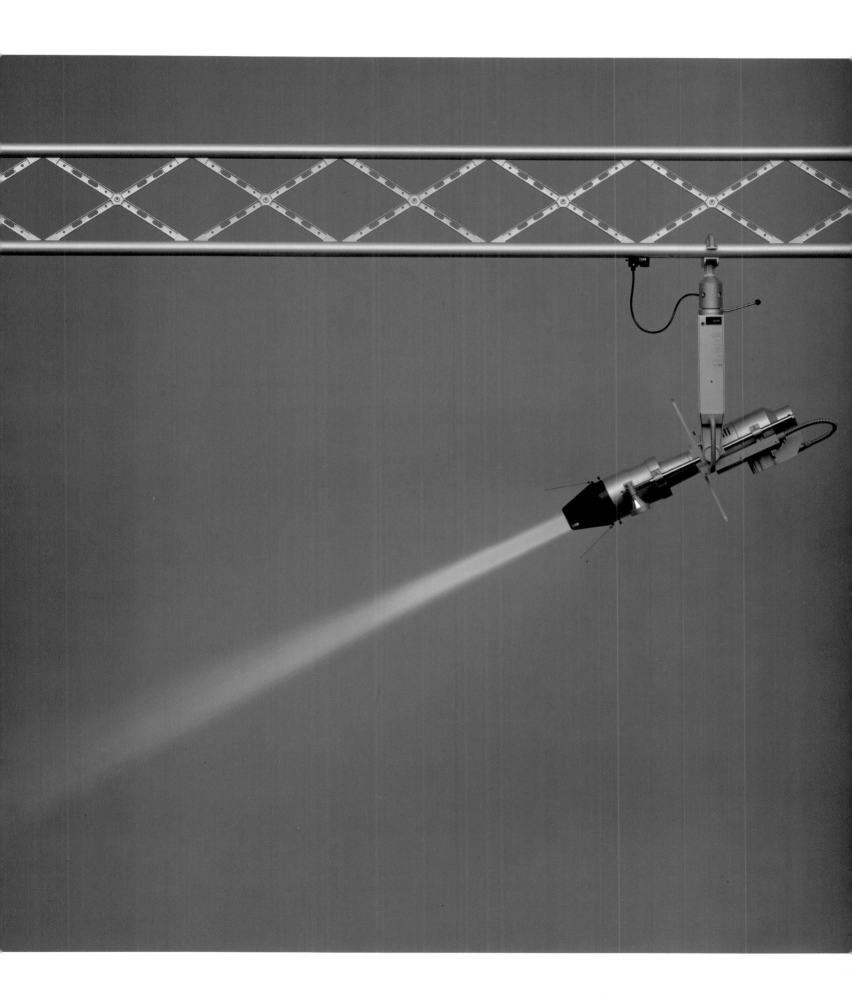

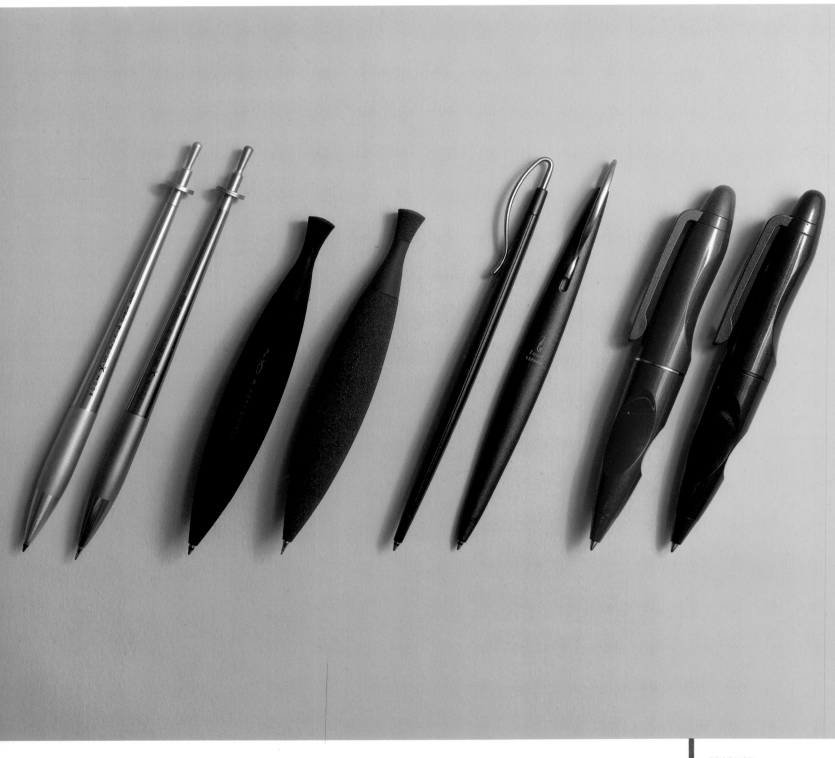

PRODUCT
Zoom Titan, Oceanic, Espana, Mano
DESIGNERS
Daniel Nebot, Luis Gonzales
MANUFACTURER
Tombow
PHOTOGRAPHER
Gail Molina

PRODUCT

Mark Maker Attache Case

DESIGNERS

Anthony J. Gentile, Cameron L. Fink, Robert W. Schram

MANUFACTURER

Sterling Marking Products Inc.

PHOTOGRAPHER

Steven Grimes

114

PRODUCT
Mystery (Portable Office)
DESIGNERS
Tibor Kalman & Douglas Riccardi
MANUFACTURER
M&Co. Labs

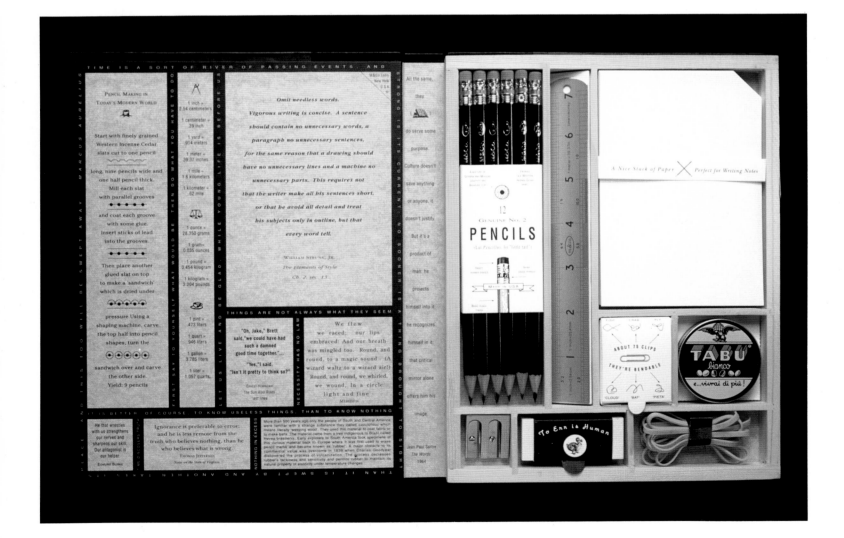

PRODUCT
Standex Collection
DESIGNERS
Satoshi Mochizuki, Naoki Hakiu
MANUFACTURER
Midori, Japan
PHOTOGRAPHER
Gail Molina

PRODUCT
Card File (Telephone)
DESIGNER
Winfried Scheuer, MA RCA
MANUFACTURER
Emform, Germany

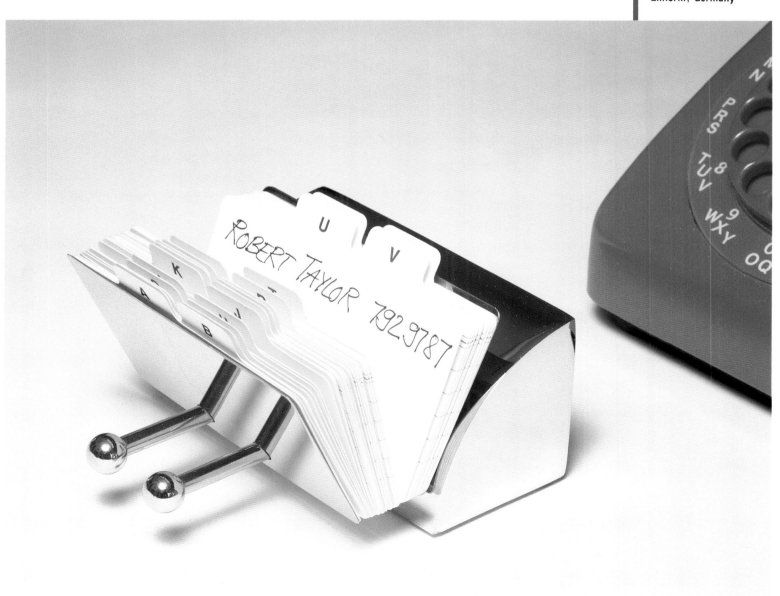

PRODUCT
The Palio Collection
DESIGNERS
**Raul De Armas and
Carolyn Iu**
MANUFACTURER
The Knoll Group
PHOTOGRAPHER
David Riley

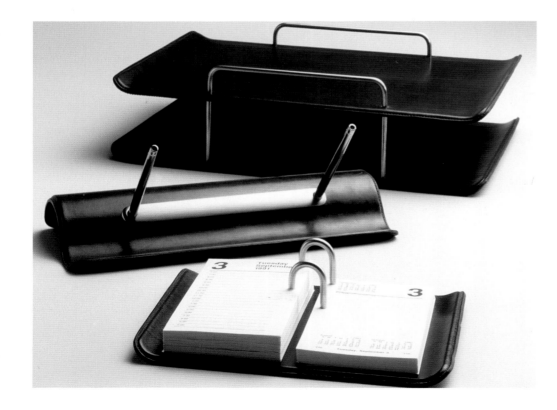

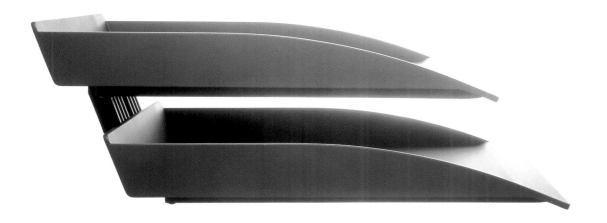

PRODUCT

**Formations Desk
Essentials**

DESIGNERS

**Eric Chan, Principal;
Federico Carandini,
Jeff Miller,
Ecco Design, Inc.**

MANUFACTURER

Evco/Atapco, St. Louis

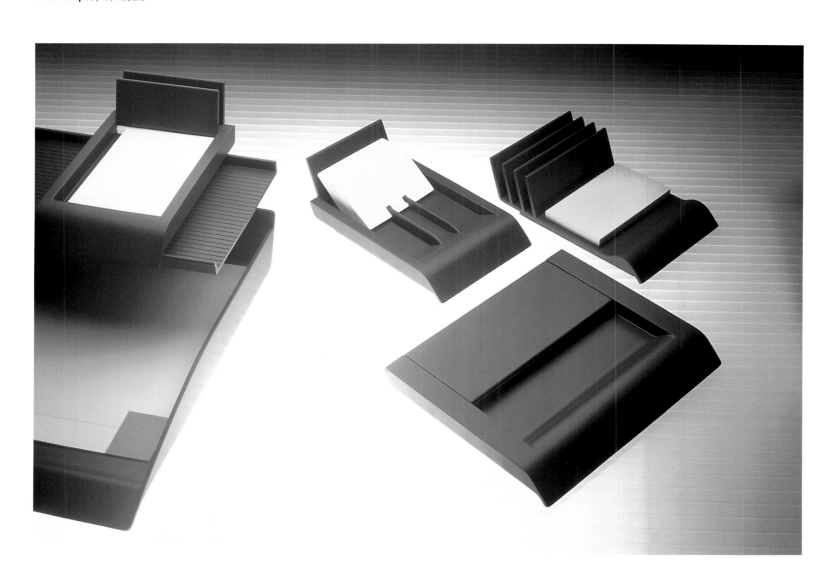

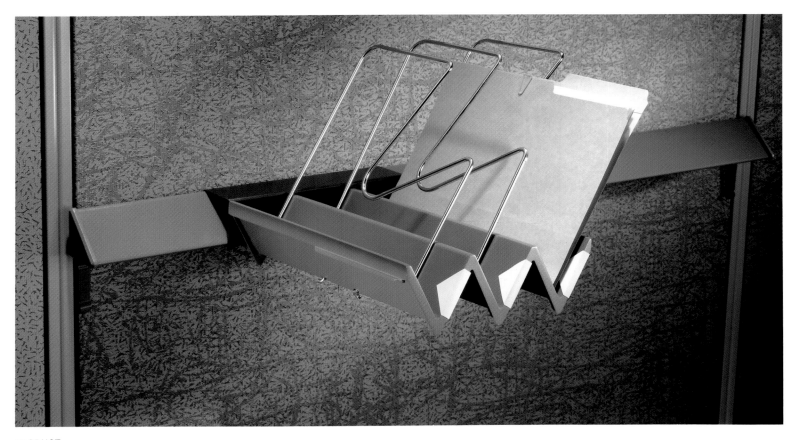

PRODUCT

WorkFlo

DESIGNER

The Richard Penney Group in collaboration with the Details Development Team

MANUFACTURER

Details—A member of the Steelcase Design Partnership

PHOTOGRAPHER

Tom Wadell

PRODUCT

Smart Label Printer Pro

DESIGNERS

John von Buelow, David Lee, Karel Slovacek

MANUFACTURER

SEIKO INSTRUMENTS USA

PHOTOGRAPHER

Terry Sutherland

PRODUCT
Savinfax 301
DESIGNERS
Andrew Serbinski, Mario Turchi
MANUFACTURER
Ricoh Company Ltd.
PHOTOGRAPHER
Mark Jenkinson

PRODUCT

**REFALO-Pockot Book
Computer**

DESIGNER

GK Incorporated

MANUFACTURER

Kyocera Corporation

PHOTOGRAPHER

Yasuhito Nakagawa

PRODUCT

**AT&T Two-Line Remote
Answering System 1332**

DESIGNER

Henry Dreyfuss Associates

MANUFACTURER

AT&T

PHOTOGRAPHER

Mikio Sekita, New York

PRODUCT

**AT&T Remote Answering
System 1523**

DESIGNERS

Henry Dreyfuss Associates

MANUFACTURER

AT&T

PHOTOGRAPHER

Mikio Sekita, New York

PRODUCT

**AT&T Portable Cellular
Telephone 3730**

DESIGNER

Henry Dreyfuss Associates

MANUFACTURER

AT&T

PHOTOGRAPHER

**Henry Dreyfuss Associates
(in-house)**

122

PRODUCT

Star Laser Printer

DESIGNERS

**Nick Barker, Loyd
Moore—Technology
Design Inc., Bellevue, WA**

MANUFACTURER

Star Micronics, Japan

PHOTOGRAPHER

Jeff Curtis

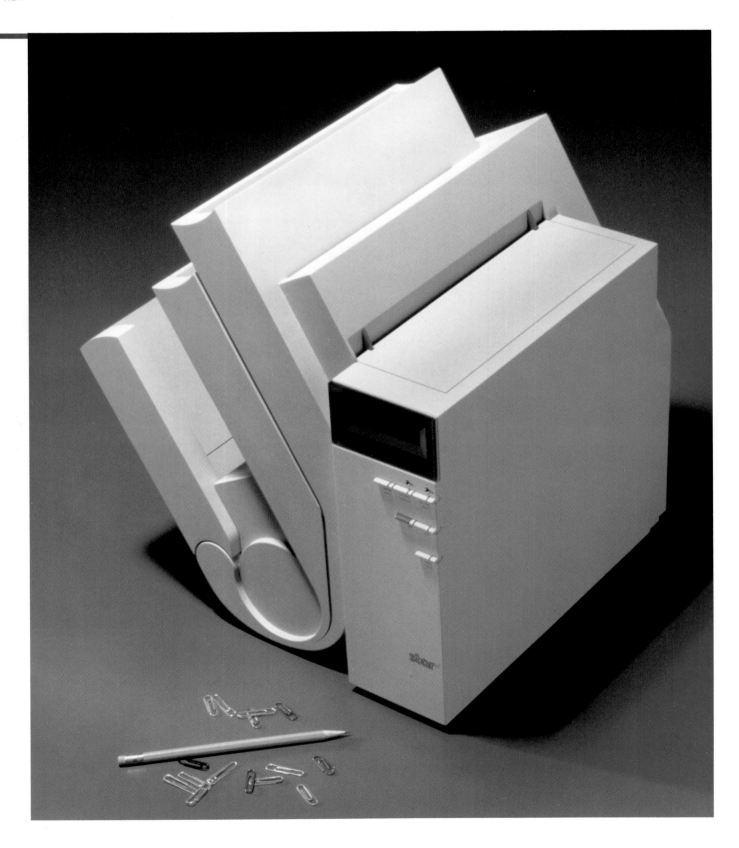

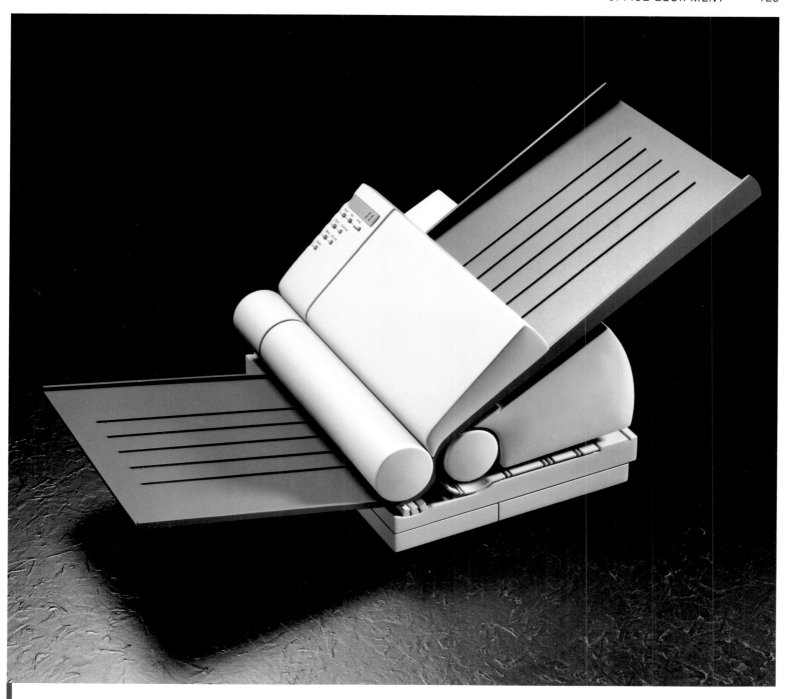

PRODUCT

Star L.C. Printer

DESIGNERS

Lloyd Moore, Oliver Grabes, Fernd van Engelen—Technology Design Inc., Bellevue, WA

MANUFACTURER

Concept Study for Star Micronics Research Corporation, Long Beach, CA

PHOTOGRAPHER

Jeff Curtis

PRODUCT

Onix Computer

DESIGNER

**John Jamieson,
Designwerks!**

MANUFACTURER

Innovative Technologies

PHOTOGRAPHER

Jeff Kamikawa

PRODUCT

**Apple Dialogue (concept)
Voice Integrated Computer
Workstation**

DESIGNER

Scott Summit

MANUFACTURER

**Student Design
Competition**

PHOTOGRAPHER

Rick English

PRODUCT

Wyse WY285

DESIGNERS

Jeff Smith, Max Yoshimoto—Lunar Joe Crosby, Frank Kula—Wyse

MANUFACTURER

Wyse Technologies

PHOTOGRAPHER

Paul Fairchild

PRODUCT

Trigem 386SX Laptop Computer

DESIGNERS

**Lunar Design
Industrial Designers: Max Yoshimoto, Robert Brunner, Gil Wong
Product Designers: Braxton Lathrop, Keith Willows, Gerard Furbershaw, Marieke Van Wijnen
Design Principal: Bill Evans
Function Engineering
Product Designers: Sung Kim, Gregor Berkowitz— Trigem Corp.
Tae Lee, Project Manufacturer**

MANUFACTURER

Trigem Corp.

PHOTOGRAPHER

Rick English

PRODUCT

**Future System Concept
2000 Mainframe Computer**

DESIGNERS

**John Guenther, Brett
Lovelady**

MANUFACTURER

Tandem Computers, Inc.

PHOTOGRAPHER

Vince Lindeman

PRODUCT

4500 Disk Subsystem

DESIGNER

**Gene Yanku and In-house
Industrial Design
Department**

MANUFACTURER

Tandem Computers, Inc.

PHOTOGRAPHERS

**Vincent Lindeman,
Jim Howell**

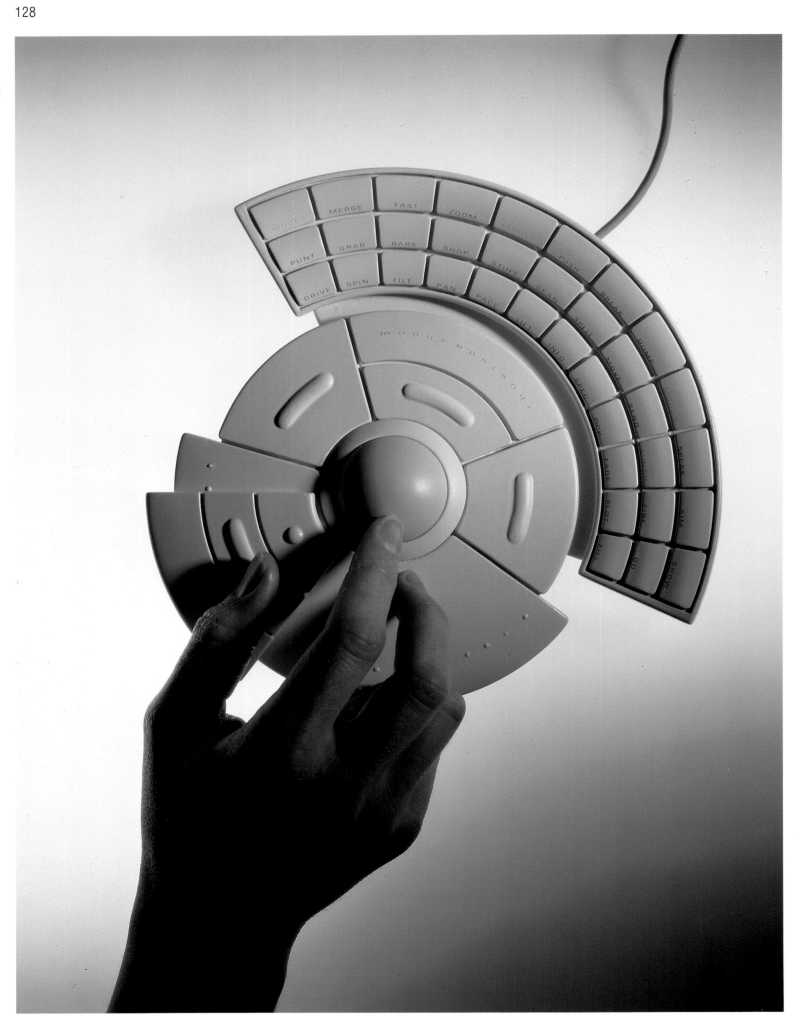

PRODUCT

M.O. Centralized Input Device

DESIGNERS

Brett Lovelady, Industrial Designer; Jeff Smith, Design Principal—Lunar Design
Jim Leftwich, Principal, Interaction Designer—Leftwich Design

MANUFACTURER

Lunar Design Incorporated

PHOTOGRAPHER

Paul Fairchild

PRODUCT

DataMyte 9000

DESIGNERS

Dan Cunagin, Eric Mueller, Eugene Reshanov

MANUFACTURER

DataMyte Corporation

PHOTOGRAPHER

Stan Waldhauser

PRODUCT

"TP 8000 Concentrator"

DESIGNERS

Paul Mulhauser, Dan Dielius—Human Factors Industrial Design, Inc.

MANUFACTURER

Telenet (A US Sprint Company)

PHOTOGRAPHER

Alex Layman

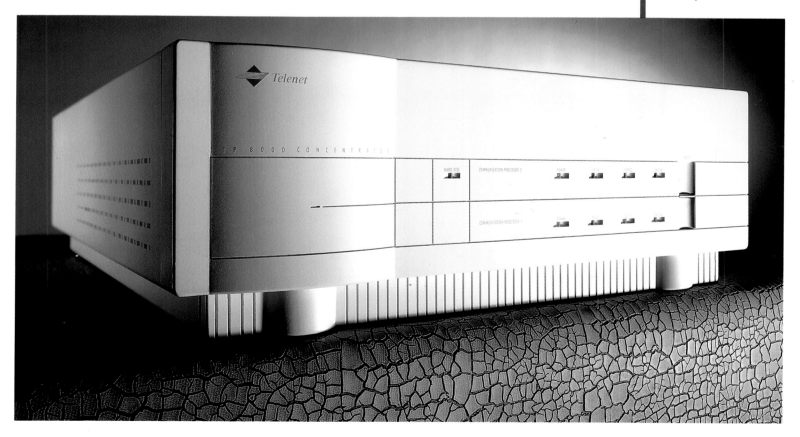

PRODUCT

**Paper Burster/Trimmer
(BT)**

DESIGNERS

**Victor Cheung, IDSA, Amy
Potts, IDSA and Tom
Devlin**

MANUFACTURER

Curtis Manufacturing

PHOTOGRAPHER

David Shopper

PRODUCT

Dimension ™ **Multi-loop Process Controller**

DESIGNERS

Eugene Reshanov, Johennes Gaston

MANUFACTURER

Research, Inc.

PHOTOGRAPHER

Stan Waldhauser

PRODUCT

Sliklink

DESIGNERS

Andrew Serbinski, Mario Turchi

MANUFACTURER

Machineart Experimental

PHOTOGRAPHER

Mark Jenkinson

PRODUCT

**POPcycle human-powered
automobile**

DESIGNERS

**Lisa Krohn and Christian
Dufay, 1991**

MANUFACTURER

Prototype by designers

PHOTOGRAPHER

Tucker Viemeister

PRODUCT
BLASTER All-terrain-vehicle
DESIGNER
GK Dynamics Incorporated
MANUFACTURER
Yamaha Motor Co., LTD

PRODUCT
V-MAX-4 Snow Mobile
DESIGNER
GK Dynamics Incorporated
MANUFACTURER
Yamaha Motor Co., LTD

PRODUCT

Morpho II Motorcycle

DESIGNER

GK Dynamics Incorporated

MANUFACTURER

Yamaha Motor Co., LTD

PHOTOGRAPHER

**Hoashi 84 Studio
Incorporated**

PRODUCT
Flarecraft 370
DESIGNER
David Wiener—David Wiener Ventures
MANUFACTURER
Flarecraft Corporation, Westport, CT
PHOTOGRAPHER
David Wiener

PRODUCT

**IDSA 1990 Conference
Surfboard (used as a
promotional item)**

DESIGNERS

**Daniel Ashcraft,
Terry Scott**

MANUFACTURER

Chuck Dent Surfboards

PHOTOGRAPHER

Tony Garcia

PRODUCT

"Playback" Folding Bicycle

DESIGNER

GK Tech Incorporated

MANUFACTURER

Maruishi Cycling Industries, LTD

PHOTOGRAPHER

Senshu Photo-Studio

PRODUCT

"Black Eagle ET-DP" Down Hill Bicycle

DESIGNER

GK Tech Incorporated

MANUFACTURER

Maruishi Cycling Industries, LTD

PHOTOGRAPHER

Senshu Photo-Studio

138

PRODUCT

"Sharkbite Kit"

DESIGNERS

Ravi Sawhney, Don Brown, Alvin Tolosa— RKS Design

MANUFACTURER

Sharkbite Velo Accessories

PHOTOGRAPHER

Ravi Sawhney

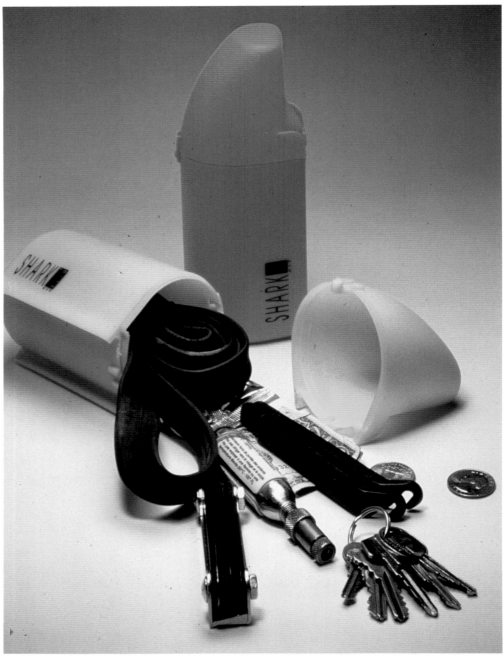

PRODUCT
Traveller Beverage Flask
DESIGNER
SIGG
MANUFACTURER
SIGG, Switzerland
PHOTOGRAPHER
Gail Molina

PRODUCT
Traveller Cycle + Sport Flask
DESIGNER
SIGG
MANUFACTURER
SIGG
PHOTOGRAPHER
Gail Molina

PRODUCT

**Airdyne Interactive
Computer Head**

DESIGNERS

**Luc Heiligenstein,
Francois Geneve, Stephen
Melamed and Richard
Riback**

MANUFACTURER

**Schwinn Cycling &
Fitness, Chicago, IL**

PHOTOGRAPHER

John Payne

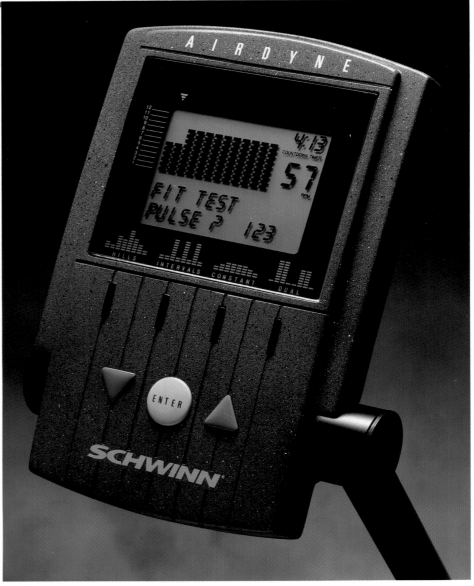

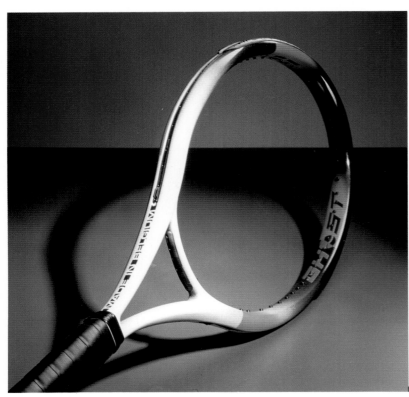

PRODUCT

''GHOST'' tennis raquet

DESIGNERS

**Design Board/Behaeghel
& Partners
Shape, C. Blin
Graphics, E. Vantal**

MANUFACTURER

**Donnay International,
Belgium**

PRODUCT

Navigator's Yeoman

DESIGNERS

**IDEO Product
Development:
Nick Dormon—Senior
Designer
Suzy Stone—Detail
Engineering Designer
Roger Penn/Jorge
Davies—Modelmaking
Development**

MANUFACTURER

**Yeoman Marine (Qubit
Group)**

PRODUCT

**Telex Pro-Star Wireless
System**

DESIGNERS

**James Luther, Eugene
Reshanov**

MANUFACTURER

**Telex Communications,
Inc.**

PHOTOGRAPHER

Stan Waldhauser

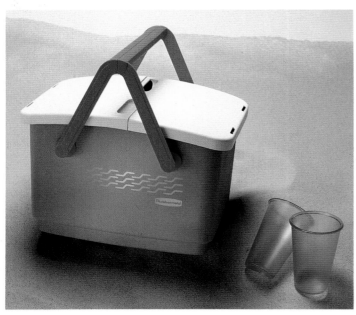

PRODUCT

Picnic Basket

DESIGNERS

**Diana Juratovac, Rainer
Teurfel**

MANUFACTURER

Rubbermaid

PHOTOGRAPHER

Larry Friar

PRODUCT
Fishing Reel ''80''
DESIGNERS
Ramon Benedito
Maite Prat
MANUFACTURER
Carretes Sagarra, S.A.
PHOTOGRAPHER
Francesc Arno

PRODUCT
Playing Cards
DESIGNER
Donald Sultan
MANUFACTURER
**Bicycle Playing Card Co.
Published by A/D,
New York**
PHOTOGRAPHER
Ken Schles

PRODUCT
"Too Pool"
DESIGNER
Allen Miesner
MANUFACTURER
Miesner Design

PRODUCT

Pentax Z-1 Camera with SMC Pentax FA Zoom 28mmF4-105mmF5.6

DESIGNER

Industrial Design Department (Pentax)

MANUFACTURER

Asahi Optical Co., Ltd.

PRODUCT

Minolta Instant Pro/ Polaroid Spectra Pro Camera

DESIGNER

Henry Dreyfuss Associates

MANUFACTURER

Polaroid

PHOTOGRAPHER

Henry Dreyfuss Associates (in-house)

PRODUCT

Digital Drums DD-6

DESIGNER

**Yamaha Product Design
Laboratory**

MANUFACTURER

Yamaha Corporation

PRODUCT

Music Sequencer QY10

DESIGNER

**Yamaha Product Design
Laboratory**

MANUFACTURER

Yamaha Corporation

PRODUCT

E-Mu Proteus Master Performance Keyboard

DESIGNERS

**Matt Barthelemy, Brett Lovelady—Industrial Design
Marieke Van Wijnen, Keith Willows, Bill Evans—Product Design
Gerard Fubershaw—Principal**

MANUFACTURER

E-mu Systems

PHOTOGRAPHER

Rick English

PRODUCT

Eldepryl Pill Dispenser

DESIGNER

**Matthew Coe,
PharmaDesign Inc.**

MANUFACTURER

PharmaDesign Inc.

PHOTOGRAPHER

Joanne Tuchrello

PRODUCT
Pascal Sterilizing/
Disinfecting Tray
DESIGNER
Frank Hosick Design
MANUFACTURER
Pascal, Inc.
PHOTOGRAPHER
Mark Wyngat

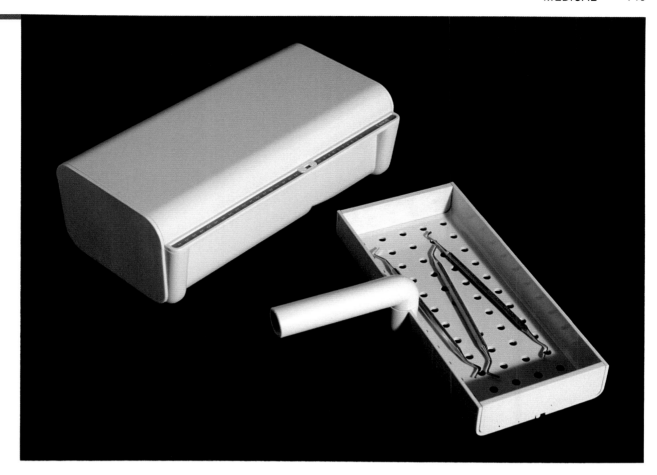

PRODUCT
Perio Pik
DESIGNER
Rainer Teufel
MANUFACTURER
Teledyne WaterPik
PHOTOGRAPHER
Larry Friar

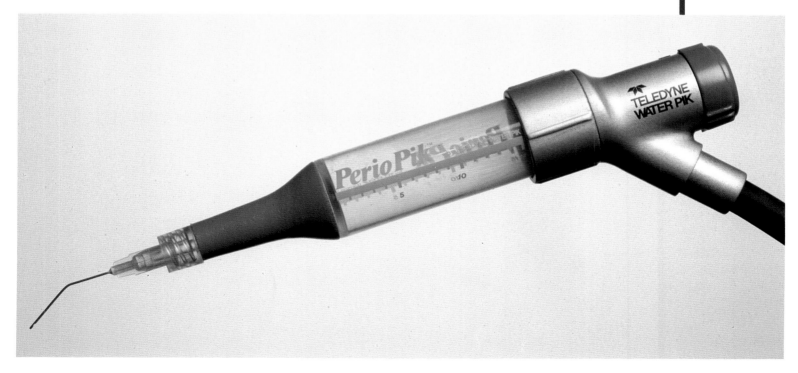

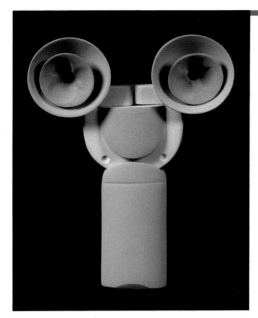

PRODUCT
Expressions Breast Pump
DESIGNER
Karen Kraus
PHOTOGRAPHER
Karen Kraus

PRODUCT
**Newport ™ Extended
Wear Cervical Collar**
DESIGNERS
**Joseph Kemme, Geoffrey
Garth, Charlie Patterson**
MANUFACTURER
**California Medical
Products, Inc., A Laerdal
Company**
PHOTOGRAPHERS
**Charlie Patterson,
Bart André**

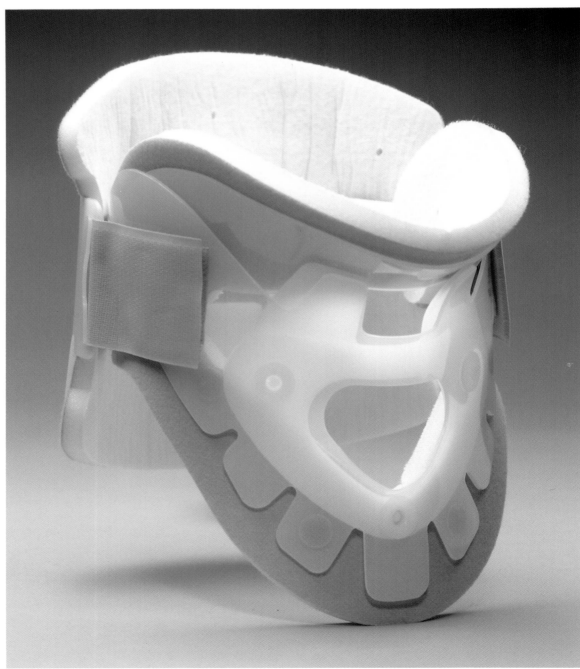

PRODUCT

**Ultima 2000 Portable
Ophthalmic Argon Laser**

DESIGNERS

**Lunar Design:
Max Yoshimoto, Industrial
Designer
Gil Wong, Industrial
Designer
Bill Evans, Industrial
Design Project Manager
Keith Willows, Product
Designer
Paul Hamerton-Kelly,
Product Designer
Gerard Furbershaw,
Product Design Project
Manager
Coherent:
Dave Youngquist, Project
Manager
Peter Keenan, Engineering
Manager**

MANUFACTURER

Coherent Medical

PHOTOGRAPHER

Paul Fairchild

PRODUCT

**Acuson Transesophageal
Probe**

DESIGNERS

**Lunar Design:
Dave Laituri, Designer
Jeff Smith, Design
Principal
Acuson:
Rich Henderson, Industrial
Design
Dave Burris, Mechanical
Engineer
Gabrielle Bungardt,
Designer**

MANUFACTURER

Acuson

PHOTOGRAPHER

Rick English

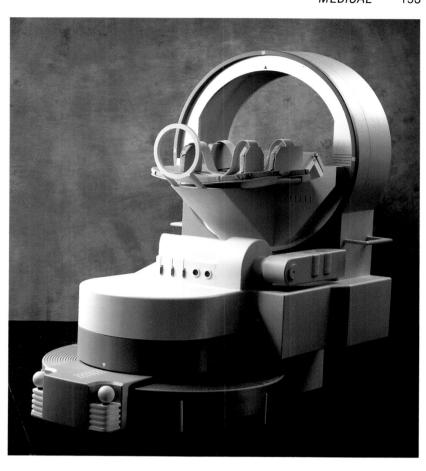

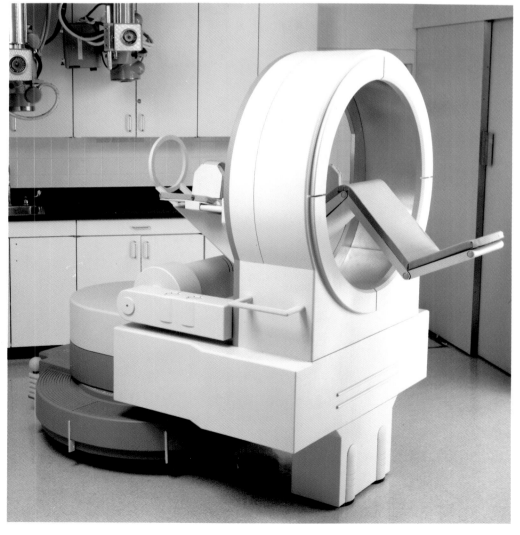

PRODUCT

Patient Positioning System (PPS)

DESIGNERS

Victor Cheung, IDSA and Amy Potts, IDSA

MANUFACTURER

Product Genesis for Massachusetts General Hospital

PHOTOGRAPHER

David Shopper

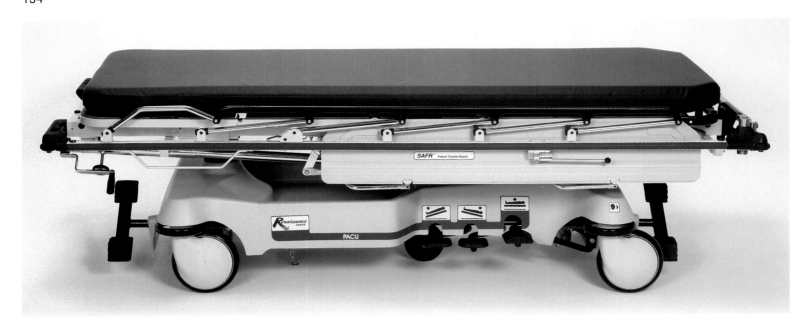

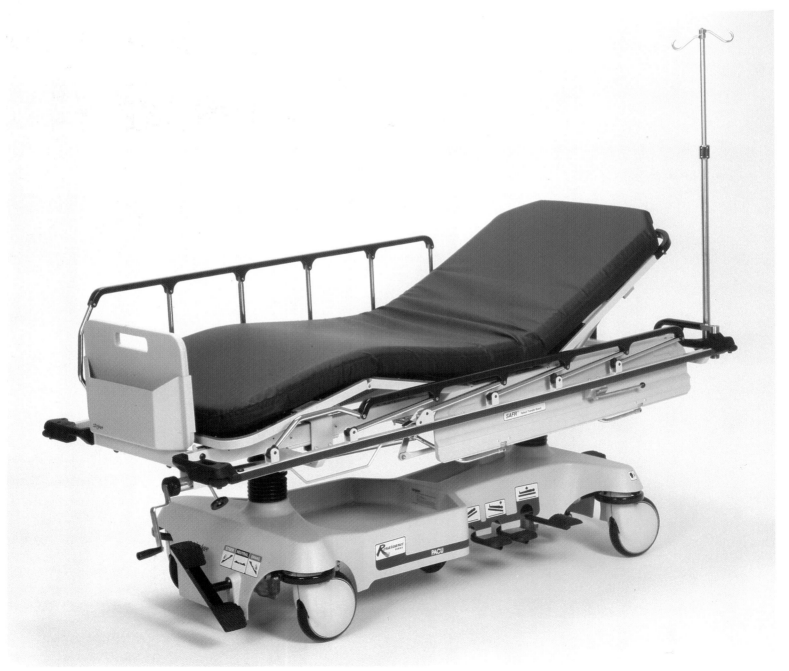

PRODUCT

**Emergency Dept./Post
Anesthesia Recovery Unit
Stretcher**

DESIGNERS

**Thomas Roney, A&R
Industrial Design
Martin Stryker, Stryker
Medical Corp.**

MANUFACTURER

**Stryker Medical
Corporation**

PHOTOGRAPHER

Lou Hands

PRODUCT

**Chairman 2000, Dental
Chair**

DESIGNER

Rainer Teufel

MANUFACTURER

**Pelton & Crane, a Division
of Siemens**

PHOTOGRAPHER

Larry Friar

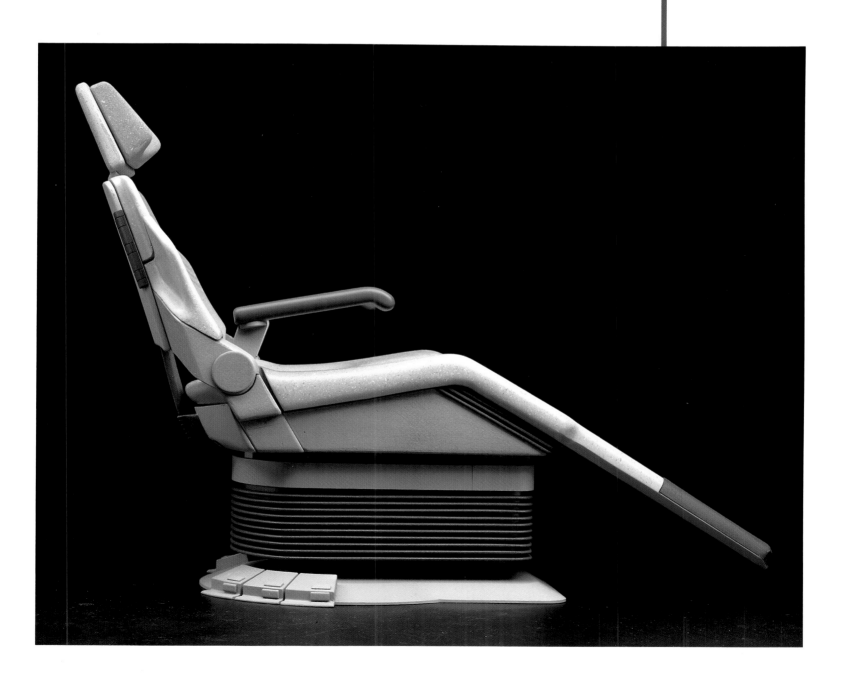

PRODUCT

OmniMed ™ Ophthalmic Laser

DESIGNERS

Edwin Beck, Gavin Jewell—Polymer Solutions, Inc.

MANUFACTURER

Summit Technology

PHOTOGRAPHER

Peter Kaskons Studio

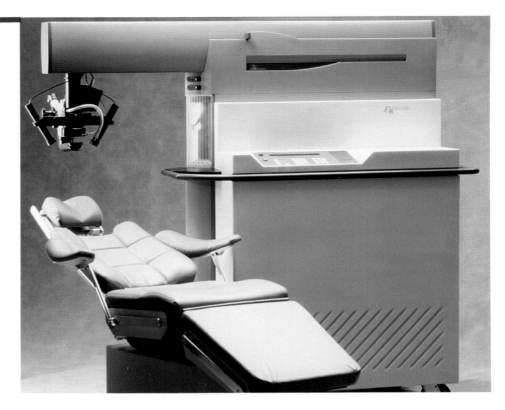

PRODUCT

TOASFLEX FT-01 Multipurpose Table

DESIGNERS

Design Soken Hiroshima Inc.

MANUFACTURER

Toas Corporation

PHOTOGRAPHER

Nissyo Iwasaki

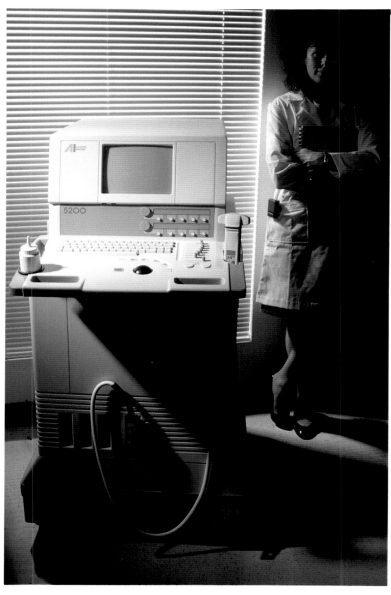

PRODUCT

**AI 5200 Ultrasound
Scanner System**

DESIGNER

**Roy Fischer—Designology
Inc.**

MANUFACTURER

Acoustic Imaging Inc.

PHOTOGRAPHER

Ralph Rippe

PRODUCT

Phased Array Scan Head

DESIGNERS

**LeRoy J. LaCelle,
Principal
Greg Marting, Industrial
Designer
Peter Pawluskiewicz,
Mechanical Designer
(ATL)**

MANUFACTURER

**Advanced Technology
Laboratories (ATL)**

PHOTOGRAPHER

Burton Irwin Photography

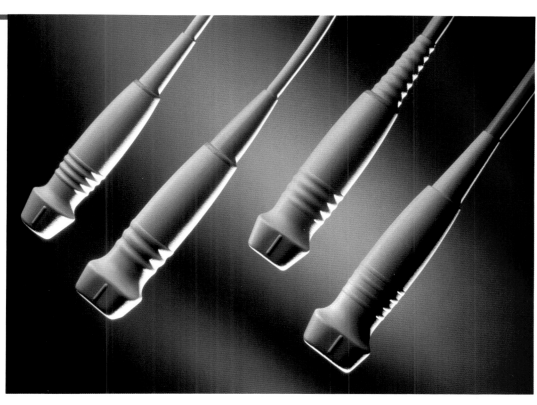

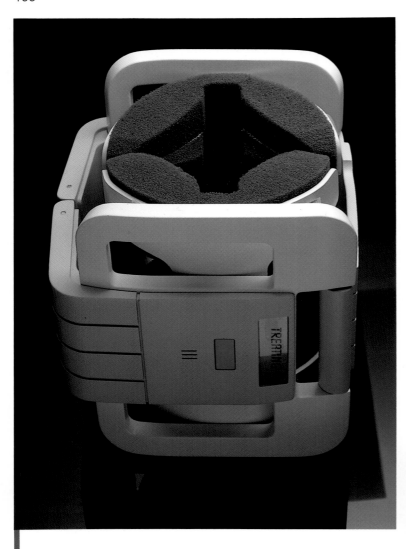

PRODUCT

LaserLink HS Slit Lamp Adapter

DESIGNERS

Max Yoshimoto, Gil Wong—Industrial Designers
Bill Evans, Industrial Design Project Manager
Paul Hamerton-Kelly, Product Design
Gerard Furbershaw, Product Design Project Manager
Coherent:
Mike Hmelar, Project Manager
Peter Keenan, Engineering Manager

MANUFACTURER

Coherent Medical

PHOTOGRAPHER

Paul Fairchild

PRODUCT

"OrthoLogic 1000" Tissue Repair Stimulator

DESIGNERS

Bert Heinzelman, Don Lamond, James Toleman, Bob Pandorf—Human Factors Industrial Design, Inc.

MANUFACTURER

OrthoLogic Corp., Phoenix, AZ

PHOTOGRAPHER

John Moldauer

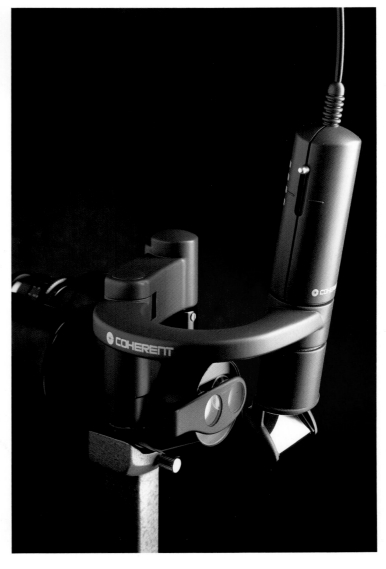

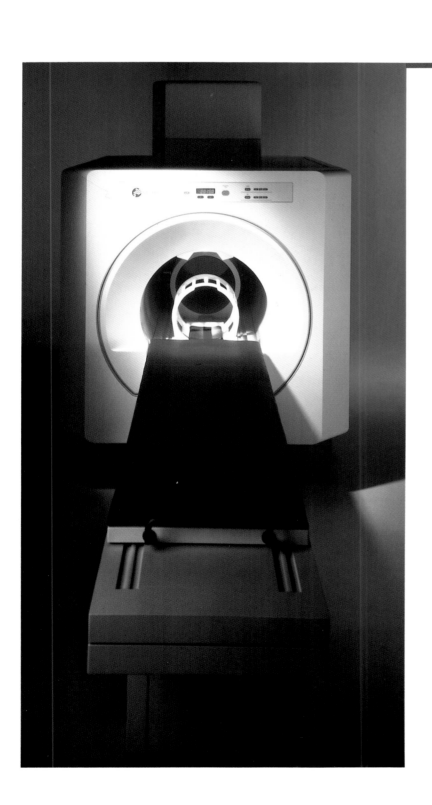

PRODUCT

OE 1.5 Magnetic Resonance Imaging (MRI) System

DESIGNERS

Bert Heinzelman, Chris Brooks, Mark Steiner, Skip Kirk, Jeff Karg— Human Factors Industrial Design, Inc.

MANUFACTURER

Otsuka Electronics (USA) Inc., Ft. Collins, CO

PHOTOGRAPHER

Tim O'Hara

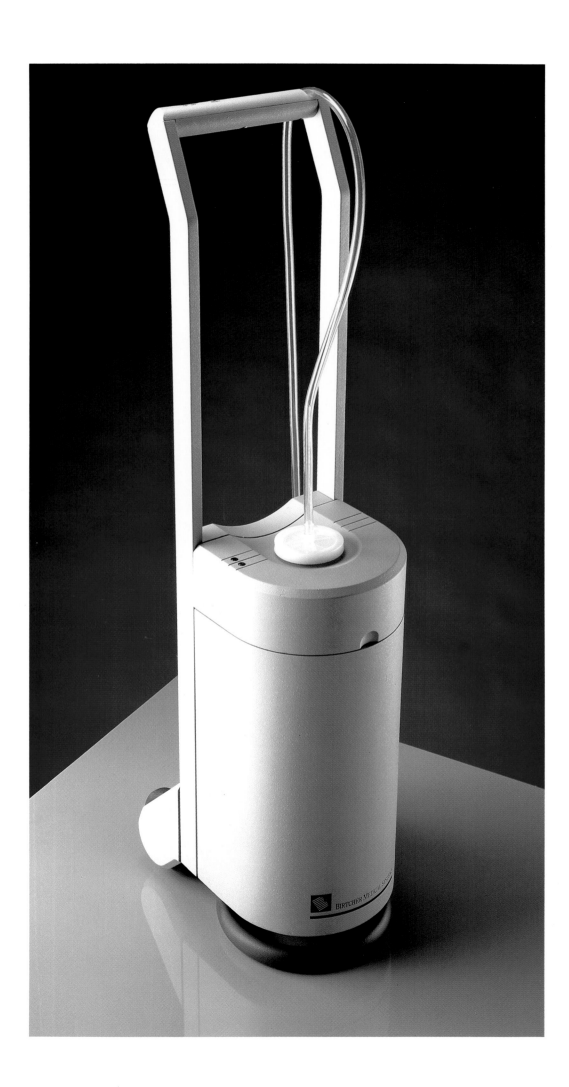

PRODUCT
Smoke Evacuator
DESIGNER
Allan Cameron
MANUFACTURER
Birtcher Medical Systems
PHOTOGRAPHER
Terry Sutherland

PRODUCT

Bio-flo Monitor

DESIGNERS

**LeRoy J. LaCelle,
Principal
Greg Marting, Industrial
Designer
Kurt Stewart, Mechanical
Engineer**

MANUFACTURER

Bio-flo

PHOTOGRAPHER

Burton Irwin Photography

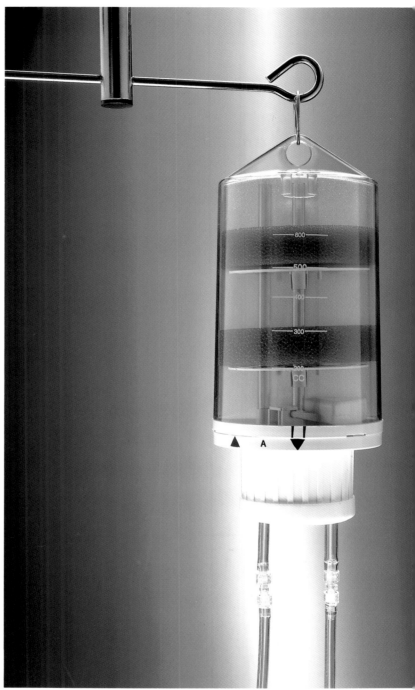

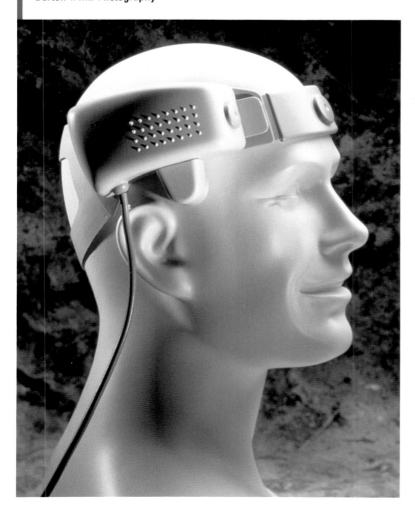

PRODUCT

**''BioSurge'' Blood
Autotransfusion Device**

DESIGNERS

**Skip Kirk, Douglas
Spranger—Human Factors
Industrial Design, Inc.
Dr. Ken Ouriel—BioSurge**

MANUFACTURER

**BioSurge, Inc., Rochester,
New York**

PHOTOGRAPHER

John Moldauer

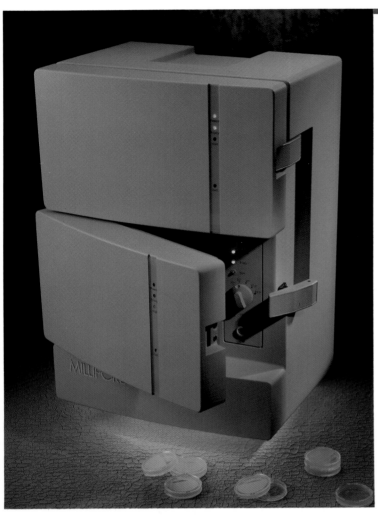

PRODUCT

Nucleus Analyzer

DESIGNER

Guy Rodomista and Alpha Products Group

MANUFACTURER

Nova Biomedical

PRODUCT

Intensive Care Patient Monitor

DESIGNERS

Bert Heinzelman, Douglas Spranger, Don Lamond— Human Factors Industrial Design, Inc.

MANUFACTURER

PPG Hellige, GMBH

PHOTOGRAPHER

Alex Layman

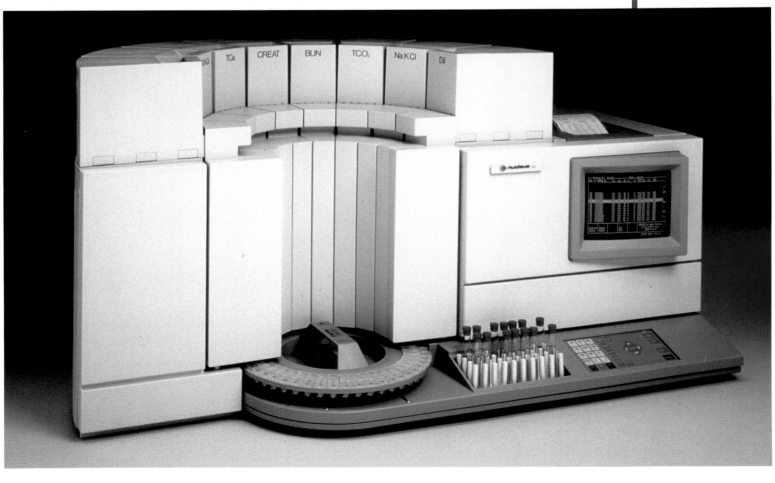

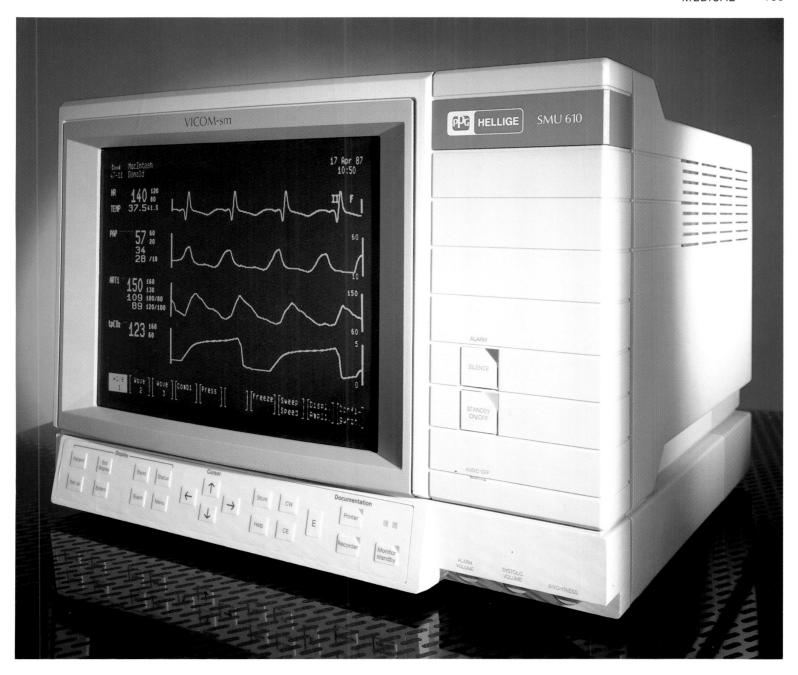

PRODUCT

Environmental Incubator

DESIGNERS

Matt Bantly, Kathryn McEntee

MANUFACTURER

Millipore Corporation

PHOTOGRAPHER

Gary Arruda, Gary Arruda Photography

PRODUCT

SCG-2000
Seismocardiograph

DESIGNERS

Tighe Belden, Dan
Cunagin, Eric Mueller,
Eugene Reshanov

MANUFACTURER

Seismed Instruments, Inc.

PHOTOGRAPHER

Stan Waldhauser

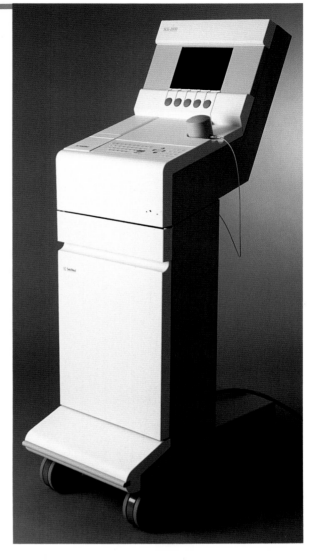

PRODUCT

''AutoTrak'' Blood
Analyzing System

DESIGNERS

Bert Heinzelman, Chris
Brooks, Don Lamond,
Mark Steiner, Human
Factors Industrial Design

MANUFACTURER

BioTek, Inc., Burlington,
VT

PHOTOGRAPHER

D. Spranger

PRODUCT

MoDic / Mobile Diagnose's Computer

DESIGNER

Neumeister Design, Munich

MANUFACTURER

BMW and MBB Gelma

PHOTOGRAPHER

Bernhard Lehn

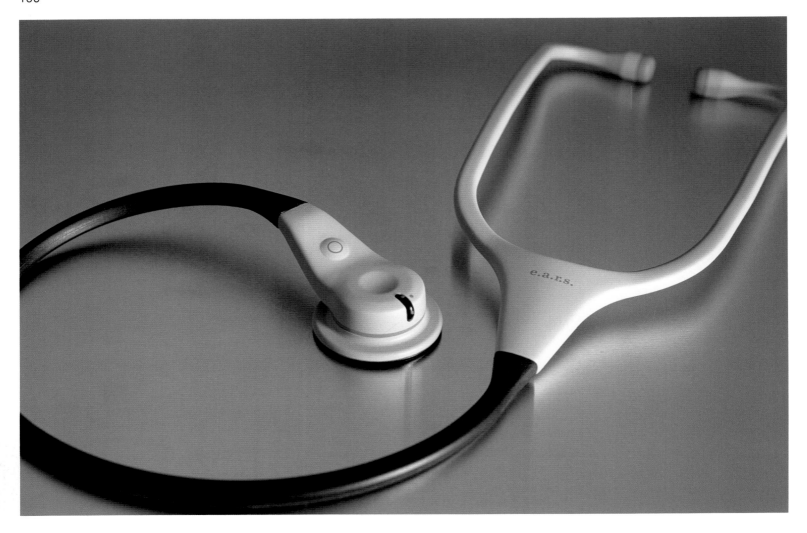

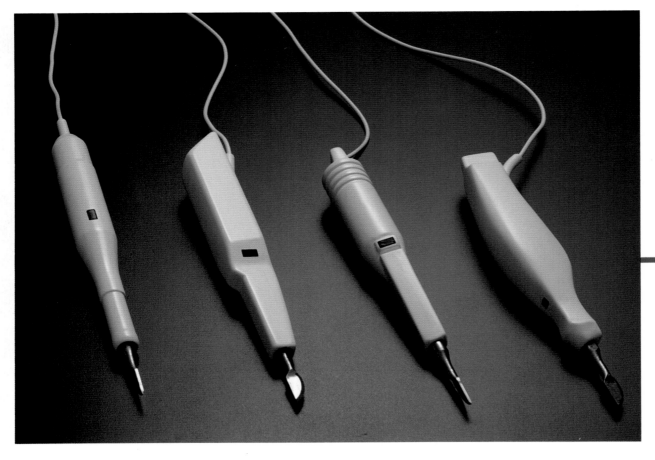

PRODUCT

Harmonic Scalpel (HS)

DESIGNERS

Victor Cheung, IDSA and Amy Potts, IDSA

MANUFACTURER

UltraCision, Inc.

PHOTOGRAPHER

Amy Potts

PRODUCT

E.A.R.S.

DESIGNERS

Roy Fischer, Randall Toltzman—Designology Inc.

MANUFACTURER

Steman & Co.

PHOTOGRAPHER

Margaret Egan

PRODUCT

"Capmix" Pre-proportion Filling Material For Dental Use

DESIGNER

Neumeister Design, Munich

MANUFACTURER

ESPE

PHOTOGRAPHER

Bernhard Lehn

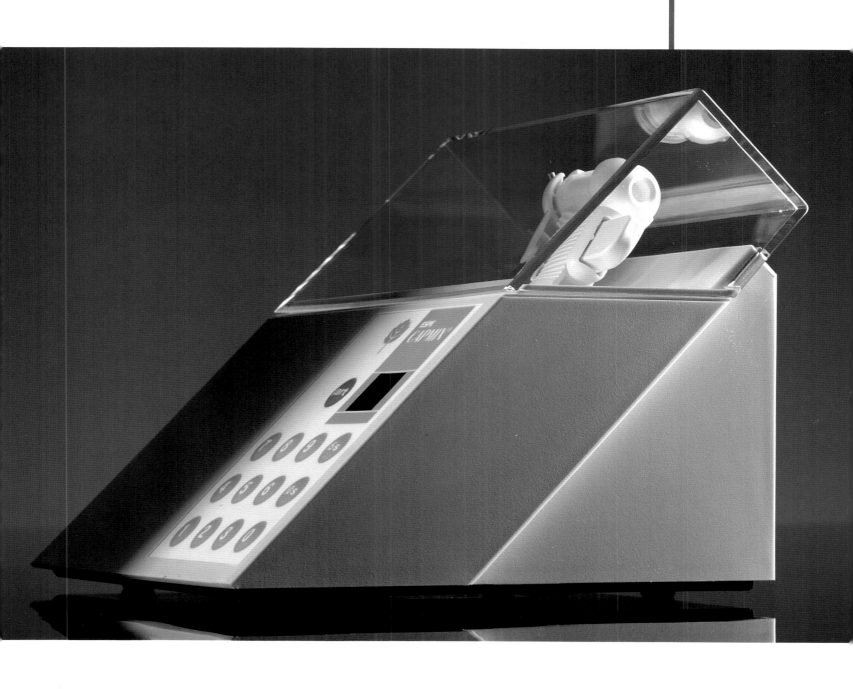

PRODUCT
''Happy Hour''
DESIGNER
**Ulrica Hydman—Vallien,
Sweden**
MANUFACTURER
Vinnasand Interieur,

Germany
PHOTOGRAPHER
Per Larsson

PRODUCT
"Honey Bee"
DESIGNER
Reiko Sudo
MANUFACTURER
NUNO Corporation

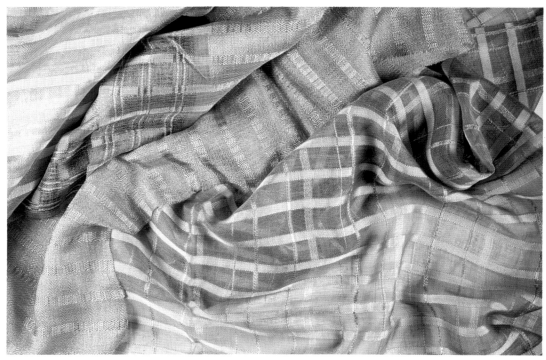

PRODUCT
Woven Textile
DESIGNER
Siñe Davidson
MANUFACTURER
Siñe Davidson
PHOTOGRAPHER
Siñe Davidson

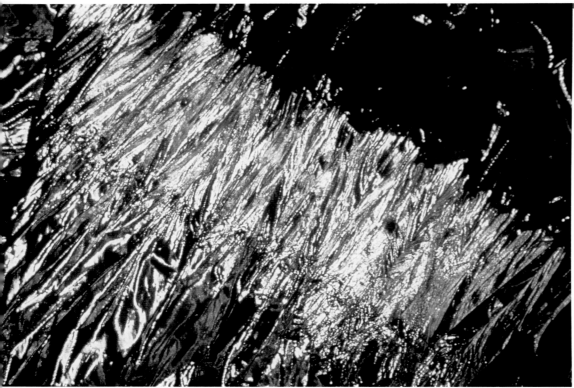

PRODUCT
**FF Cloth Big Wave Fabric
No. 9-113**
DESIGNERS
Junichi Arai
MANUFACTURER
K&T Corporation

PRODUCT
''Bittersweet''
DESIGNER
Georgia Marsh
MANUFACTURER
**Published by A/D, New
York. Printed for A/D by
Grisworld Textiles,
Westerly, Rhode Island**
PHOTOGRAPHER
Ken Scheles

PRODUCT
''Birds''
DESIGNER
Jasia Szerszynska
MANUFACTURER
Designers Guild

PRODUCT

**Basket Weave Big Pockets
Fabric No. 1-35**

DESIGNER

Junichi Arai

MANUFACTURER

NUNO Corporation

PRODUCT

**"Mondrian in Chartreuse
on a Bed of Roses and a
Flowing Dress"**

DESIGNER

**Frederic Schwartz,
Anderson/Schwartz
Architects, assisted by
Janice Kitchen**

PHOTOGRAPHER

Steve Moore

PRODUCT
"New Legends"
DESIGNER
Marc Van Hoe
MANUFACTURER
Ter Molst
PHOTOGRAPHER
Jan Kesteleyn

PRODUCT
In Gold We Trust
DESIGNER
Alfonso Sostres
MANUFACTURER
Marieta

PRODUCT
Alfombra NEKO
DESIGNER
Xano Armenter
MANUFACTURER
Marieta

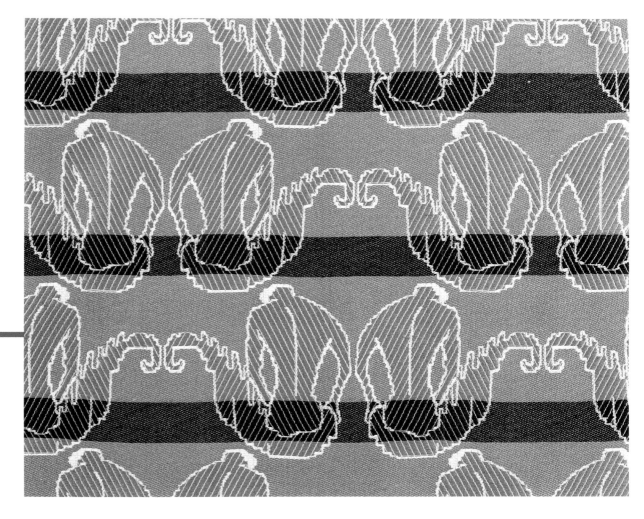

PRODUCT
''Shell''
DESIGNER
Mark Van Hoe
MANUFACTURER
Ter Molst
PHOTOGRAPHER
Jan Kesteleyn

PRODUCT
Tela BOTANICA
DESIGNER
Xano Armenter
MANUFACTURER
Marieta

PRODUCT
"Moor"
DESIGNER
Marc Van Hoe
MANUFACTURER
Ter Molst
PHOTOGRAPHER
Jan Kesteleyn

PRODUCT
FD 5703 ''Hologram''
DESIGNER
**The Development Division
of Fujie Textile Co., Ltd.**
MANUFACTURER
**Iizuka Kigyo Co., Ltd. and
Development of Fujie
Textile Co., Ltd.**
PHOTOGRAPHER
D.V.C.

PRODUCT
Alfombra RIGOLETTO
DESIGNER
Perico Pastor
MANUFACTURER
Marieta

PRODUCT
Tra-La-La Day
DESIGNER
Christine Van Der Hurd
PHOTOGRAPHER
Peter Ledwith

PRODUCT
Tra-La-La Night
DESIGNER
Christine Van Der Hurd
PHOTOGRAPHER
Peter Ledwith

180

PRODUCT
Alfombra LEON DE COCO
DESIGNER
Peret
MANUFACTURER
Marieta (Handmade)

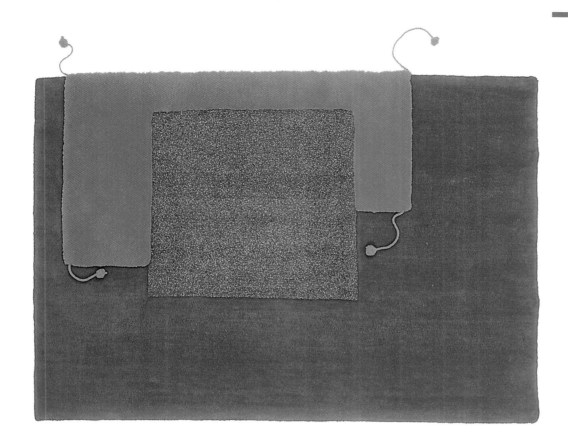

PRODUCT
"Jasmin" Rug
DESIGNER
Claude Picasso (France)
MANUFACTURER
Neotu France—Sopha Industrie

PRODUCT
"Friends" Carpet
DESIGNER
Ulrica Hydman—Vallien, Sweden
MANUFACTURER
Treger International, Sweden
PHOTOGRAPHER
Per Larsson

PRODUCT
"Star of India"
DESIGNER
Christine Van Der Hurd
PHOTOGRAPHER
Peter Ledwith

PRODUCT
Banana Aliens
DESIGNER
Christine Van Der Hurd
PHOTOGRAPHER
Peter Ledwith

PRODUCT
Kuba I
DESIGNER
Christine Van Der Hurd
PHOTOGRAPHER
Peter Ledwith

PRODUCT
''Square Dance''
DESIGNER
Vincent Carleton
MANUFACTURER
Carleton Designs
PHOTOGRAPHER
Sean Sprague

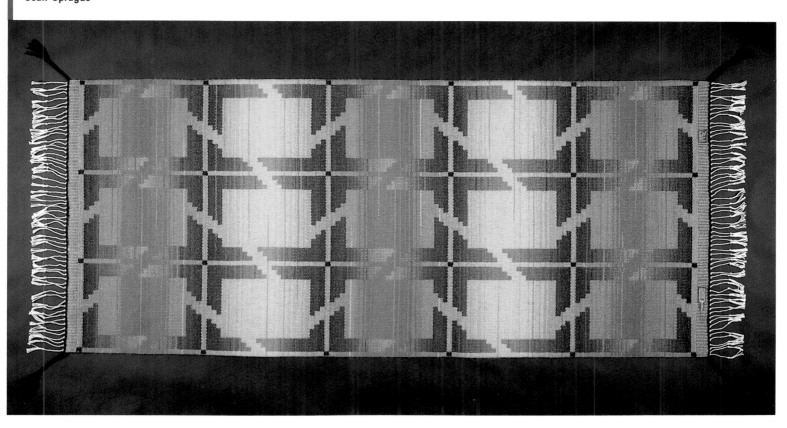

PRODUCT
**"TIGER" 1991—Goblets
and Jars**
DESIGNER
Ulrica Hydman-Vallien
MANUFACTURER
Kosta-Boda AB, Sweden

PRODUCT
**"Royal Holland"
Dinnerware**
DESIGNER
Ravage
MANUFACTURER
Archetype, New York

PRODUCT
Ocean Hand blown glass
DESIGNER
Ann Wåhlström
MANUFACTURER
Kosta Boda, Sweden
PHOTOGRAPHER
Studio Hörlin

PRODUCT
Johansfors Hand blown glass
DESIGNER
Ann Wåhlström
MANUFACTURER
Kosta Boda, Sweden
PHOTOGRAPHER
Studio Hörlin

PRODUCT
''daDa Boxes''
DESIGNER
Denis Collura
MANUFACTURER
Archetype, New York

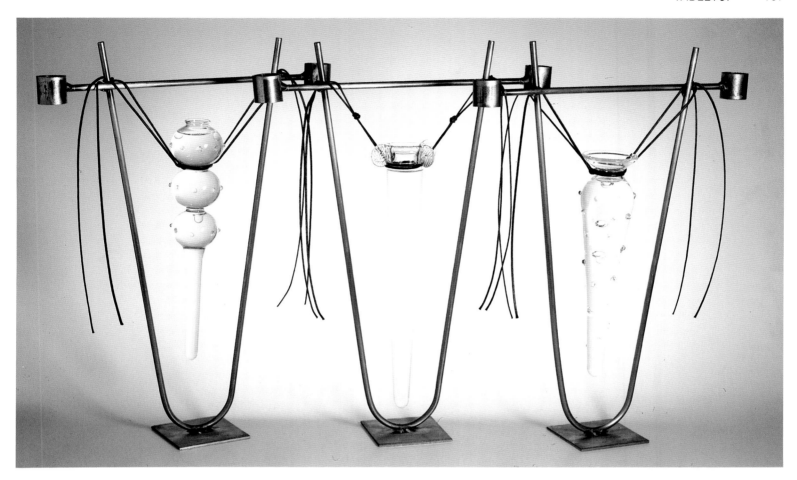

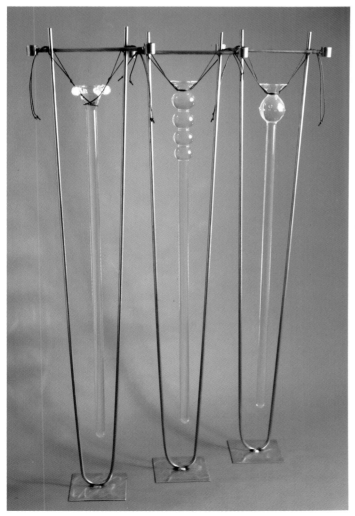

PRODUCT
Joyce Bud Vase
DESIGNER
Zev Vaughn
MANUFACTURER
Public Domain
PHOTOGRAPHER
Zev Vaughn

PRODUCT
Swinger, Male & Female Vases
DESIGNER
Studio F Kia—USA
MANUFACTURER
Studio F Kia—USA

Swinger, Male & Female Vases

PRODUCT
Nile Vase
DESIGNER
Chris Collicott
MANUFACTURER
Chris Collicott
PHOTOGRAPHER
Chris Collicott

PRODUCT

''TSUNO'' Vase

DESIGNER

Makoto Komatsu

MANUFACTURER

Product M.

DISTRIBUTOR

**Eastern Accent
International, Boston, MA**

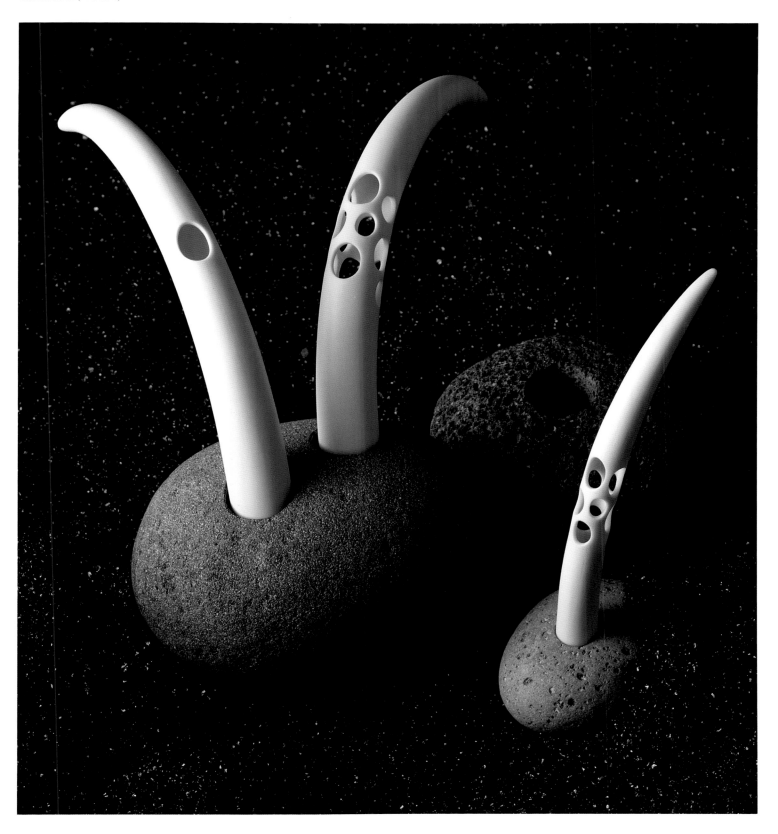

PRODUCT

Toby Russell Pewter & Metal Designs—Waterline Vase; Intersecting Vase

DESIGNERS

John Benjamin, Tobias Russell

MANUFACTURER

Roby Russell

PHOTOGRAPHER

Justin Thomas

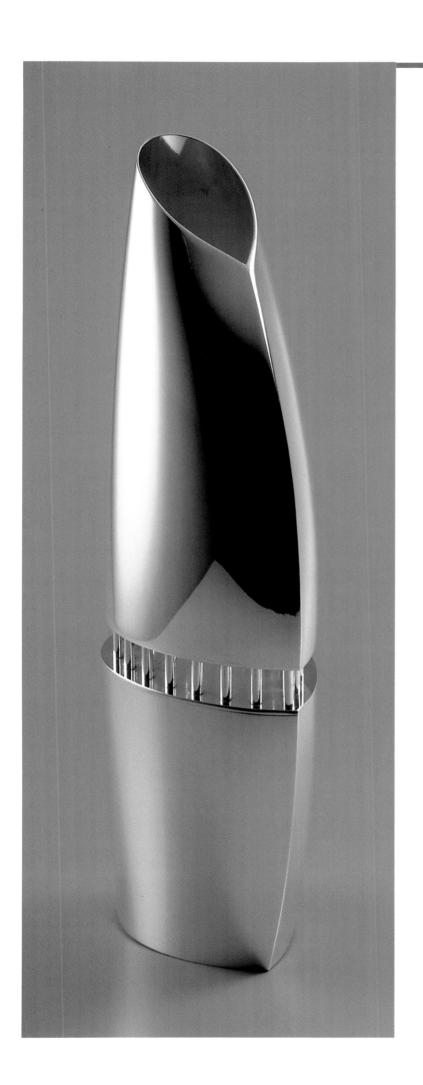

PRODUCT
Inquietante Vase
DESIGNER
Lino Sabattini
MANUFACTURER
**Sabattini Argenteria
S.P.A.**
PHOTOGRAPHER
Romano Fotografie, Italy

PRODUCT
Smitty Candlestick
DESIGNER
Ries Niemi
MANUFACTURER
Ries Niemi, Los Angeles

PRODUCT
Halley Centerpiece
DESIGNER
Lino Sabattini
MANUFACTURER
**Sabattini Argenteria
S.P.A.**
PHOTOGRAPHER
Romano Fotografie, Italy

PRODUCT
Harmony Candleholder
DESIGNER
Lino Sabattini
MANUFACTURER
**Sabattini Argenteria
S.P.A.**
PHOTOGRAPHER
Romano Fotografie, Italy

PRODUCT
Glass Candlesticks
DESIGNER
Rob Dashorst
MANUFACTURER
Daskas Amsterdam
PHOTOGRAPHER
Paul Gofferjé

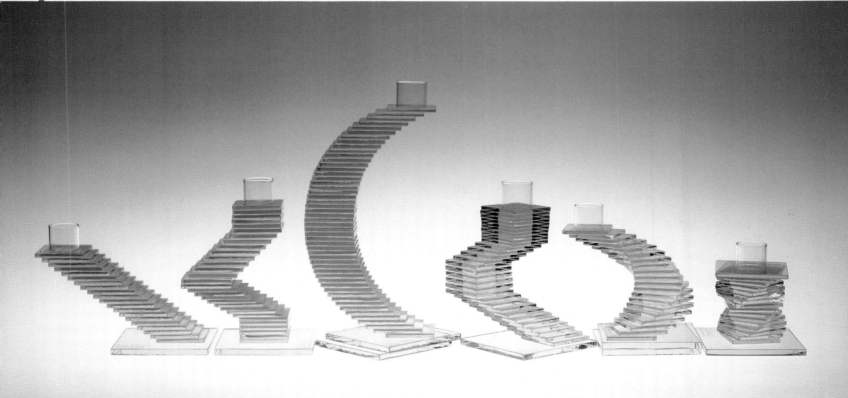

PRODUCT
"Beam"
DESIGNER
Allen Miesner
MANUFACTURER
Miesner Design

PRODUCT
Sterling Silver Candle Sticks
DESIGNER
Laura Handler, Handler
MANUFACTURER
Pomellato, S.P.A.—Milan, Italy

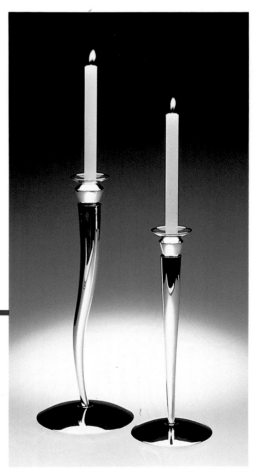

PRODUCT
Lutradur Picture Frame
DESIGNER
**David Chapin, Forma
Design**
MANUFACTURER
Freudenberg Spunweb
PHOTOGRAPHER
**Duane Salstrand,
Salstrand Photography**

PRODUCT
Frame
DESIGNER
Cal Thompson
MANUFACTURER
Archetype, New York

PRODUCT
Rocket Dish
DESIGNER
Kerr Keller
MANUFACTURER
Umbra Shades Ltd.
PHOTOGRAPHER
Chris Barnes

PRODUCT
Giostra
DESIGNER
Lino Sabattini
MANUFACTURER
**Sabattini Argenteria
S.P.A. Bregnano, Italy**
PHOTOGRAPHER
Romano Fotografie

PRODUCT
Shell Series Bowls
DESIGNER
Ann Morhauser
MANUFACTURER
Annieglass Studio
PHOTOGRAPHER
Viktor Budnik

PRODUCT
**Blown and Sand Etched
Glass Bowl**
DESIGNER
Patrick Wadley
MANUFACTURER
Archetype, New York

PRODUCT
Decorative Metal Vessels
DESIGNER
Michael Rowe
MANUFACTURER
Michael Rowe
PHOTOGRAPHERS
David Cripps, Ian Haigh

PRODUCT
"Fenice," Coffee and Tea Service
DESIGNER
Lino Sabattini
MANUFACTURER
Sabattini Argenteria S.P.A., Bregnano, Italy
PHOTOGRAPHER
Romano Fotografie

PRODUCT
Rocket Peppermill
DESIGNER
Kerr Keller
MANUFACTURER
Umbra Shades Ltd.
PHOTOGRAPHER
Chris Barnes

PRODUCT
Sterling Silver Salt and Pepper Shakers
DESIGNERS
Laura Handler, David Peschel—Handler
MANUFACTURER
Pomellato, S.P.A.—Milan, Italy

PRODUCT

Hefty Press'n Pour Pitcher

DESIGNERS

Marlan Polhemus, Andrew Alger

MANUFACTURER

Mobil Corporation / Hefty Division

PHOTOGRAPHER

Claude Cummings

PRODUCT

Thermal Carafes

DESIGNERS

Greg Breiding, Tatjana Leblanc, Bob Mervar, Michael Luh—Fitch RichardsonSmith

MANUFACTURER

Thermos

PHOTOGRAPHER

Courtesy of Thermos

PRODUCT
Hot Cooker
DESIGNER
Makoto Komatsu
MANUFACTURER
**Ceramic Japan
U.S. Representative—
Eastern Accent
International, Boston, MA**

PRODUCT
Composition Knives
DESIGNER
Olaf Göckeritz
MANUFACTURER
Giesser of Germany

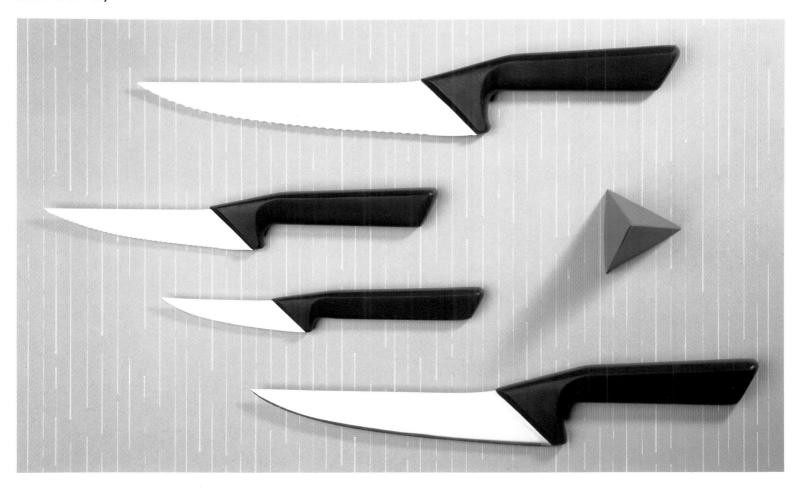

PRODUCT

**John Deere STX Suburban
LX 172 Tractor**

DESIGNER

Henry Dreyfuss Associates

MANUFACTURER

John Deere

PHOTOGRAPHER

**John Deere (Advertising
Department)**

PRODUCT

Garden Shed

DESIGNERS

Frederic Schwartz,
Eric Fiss
Anderson/Schwartz
Architects

PHOTOGRAPHER

Steve Moore

PRODUCT

Hose Reel Cart

DESIGNER

Gordon Randall Perry

MANUFACTURER

Melnor Industries

PHOTOGRAPHER

Gordon Randall Perry

PRODUCT

Roughneck Mailbox

DESIGNERS

Peter Koloski, Design Central; Keith Brightbill, Rubbermaid

MANUFACTURER

Rubbermaid

PHOTOGRAPHER

Larry Friar

PRODUCT

Charcoal Barbecue

DESIGNER

Mark Isaacs

MANUFACTURER

Prototype

PHOTOGRAPHER

Mark Isaacs

PRODUCT
Lightning Bolt Weathervane
DESIGNER
Smart Design
MANUFACTURER
The Markuse Corp.

PRODUCT
Angel Weathervane
DESIGNER
Stanley Tigerman
MANUFACTURER
The Markuse Corp.

PRODUCT
Flag Weathervane
DESIGNER
Michael Graves
MANUFACTURER
The Markuse Corp.

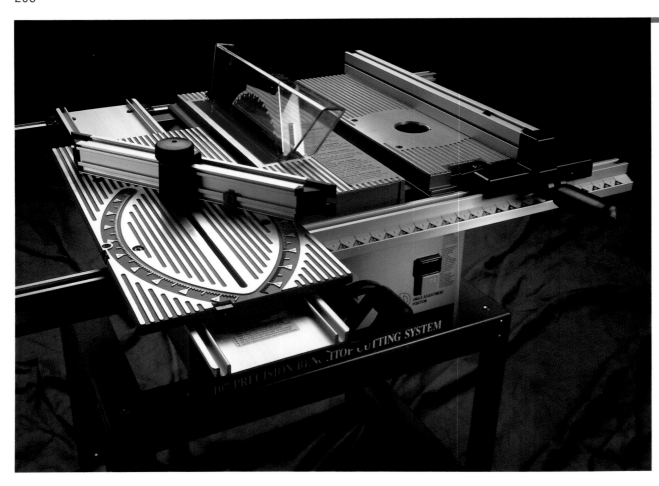

PRODUCT
Portable 10'' Table Saw
DESIGNERS
**Ed Lawing, Ken Brazell
(formerly of)—Fitch
RichardsonSmith**
MANUFACTURER
Ryobi, Ltd.
PHOTOGRAPHER
Dan Turner

PRODUCT
**Snap-on Tools Pneumatic
Sander**
DESIGNER
Renquist/Associates
MANUFACTURER
Snap-on Tools
PHOTOGRAPHER
**Renquist Associates
in-house photography**

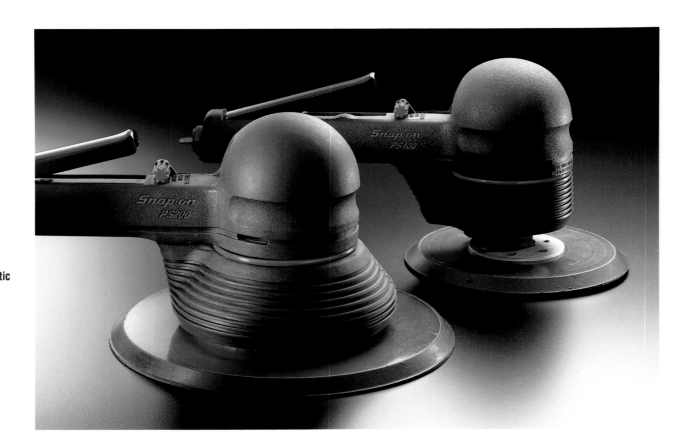

PRODUCT

Lufkin 2000 Series Tape Measures

DESIGNER

David Chapin, Forma Design

MANUFACTURER

CooperTools

PHOTOGRAPHER

Duane Salstrand, Salstrand Photography

PRODUCT

Tool Boxes

DESIGNERS

Robert J. Hayes, Spencer Murrell, Vince Haley (formerly of)—Fitch RichardsonSmith

MANUFACTURER

Rubbermaid, Inc.

PHOTOGRAPHER

Mark A. Steele, Fitch RichardsonSmith

PRODUCT

**Lufkin M-48 Ultrasonic
Measuring Device**

DESIGNER

**David Chapin, Forma
Design**

MANUFACTURER

CopperTools

PHOTOGRAPHER

**Duane Salstrand,
Salstrand Photography**

PRODUCT

Audiovox Transmitters

DESIGNERS

**Mark Dziersk, David
Harris, Tim Repp**

MANUFACTURER

Audiovox

PHOTOGRAPHER

Rick Whittey

PRODUCT
TR 211 Vacuum Sensor
DESIGNER
Gheorhe Teodorescu
MANUFACTURER
Leybold AG
PHOTOGRAPHER
M-2 Studio-Cologne

PRODUCT
Panasonic Super Light Plus
DESIGNERS
Mark Dziersk, Bill Valls
MANUFACTURER
Panasonic Industrial Company
PHOTOGRAPHER
Rick Whittey

PRODUCT
Rota Light Flashlight
DESIGNER
Frank Hosick Design
MANUFACTURER
UCO, Inc.
PHOTOGRAPHER
Robert Hay

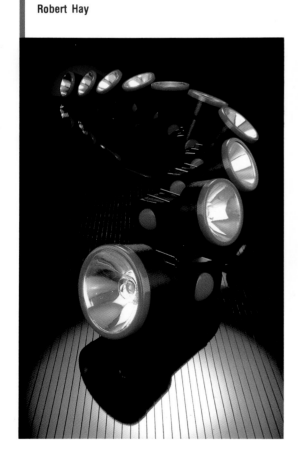

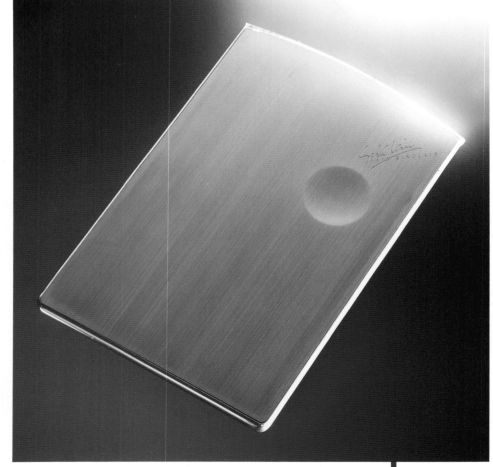

PRODUCT
Liteblade
DESIGNER
Iain Sinclair
MANUFACTURER
Iain Sinclair

PRODUCT
ZAP Torch
DESIGNER
Alan Uke
MANUFACTURER
Underwater Kinetics, USA
PHOTOGRAPHER
Gail Molina

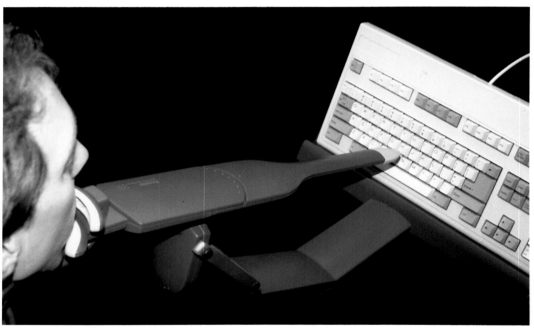

PRODUCT

Access Power • Pointer

DESIGNER

Vincent L. Haley— Design Inspiration (formerly V.H. Designs)

CLIENT

Sponsored by IBM and North Carolina State University

PHOTOGRAPHER

Vincent L. Haley

PRODUCT

Llana Rubi Trowel

DESIGNER

Joan Sunyol, Via Design, S.A.

MANUFACTURER

Germans Boada, S.A.

PHOTOGRAPHER

M.I. Marroyo

PRODUCT

Funnel and Drip Pan

DESIGNERS

Hiro Kozu, Michael Young —Michael W. Young Assoc. Inc.

MANUFACTURER

Detailed Designs, Inc., Plainfield, NJ

PHOTOGRAPHER

H. Kozu

PRODUCT

Squeegee

DESIGNERS

Hiro Kozu, Chig-Ping Hsia, Robert von Meyer, Michael Young—Michael W. Young Assoc. Inc.

MANUFACTURER

Detailed Designs, Inc., Plainfield, NJ

PHOTOGRAPHER

S.F. Lee / H. Kozu

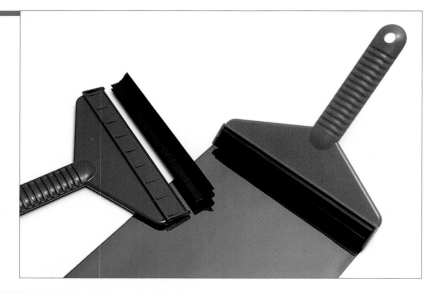

PRODUCT

"Feddy" Series of Cleaning Products

DESIGNERS

Frank R. Wilgus, Frank A. Wilgus, Inars Jurjans, Deane W. Richardson, David Laituri (formerly of), Vince Haley (formerly of) —Fitch RichardsonSmith

MANUFACTURER

Duskin Co., Ltd., Osaka, Japan

PHOTOGRAPHER

Mark A. Steele, Fitch Richardsonsmith

PRODUCT
Handi-Scratch Wire Brush
DESIGNERS
Sean Simmons, Monte Levin—Sonneman Design Group, Inc.
MANUFACTURER
Empire Brushes, Inc.
PHOTOGRAPHER
Stanley K. Patz

PRODUCT

Spenser (dry fabric softener-dryer sheet dispenser)

DESIGNERS

Dean Bidwell, Kent Olsen, Oliver Grabes—Technology Design, Inc., Bellevue, WA

MANUFACTURER

Spenser Corporation, Seattle, WA

PHOTOGRAPHER

Doug Ogle

PRODUCT

Body Conscious Lotion

DESIGNERS

Laura Handler—Handler James Gager, Senior Vice President and Creative Director—Prescriptives World Wide

MANUFACTURER

Prescriptives

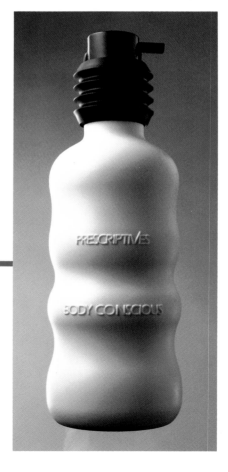

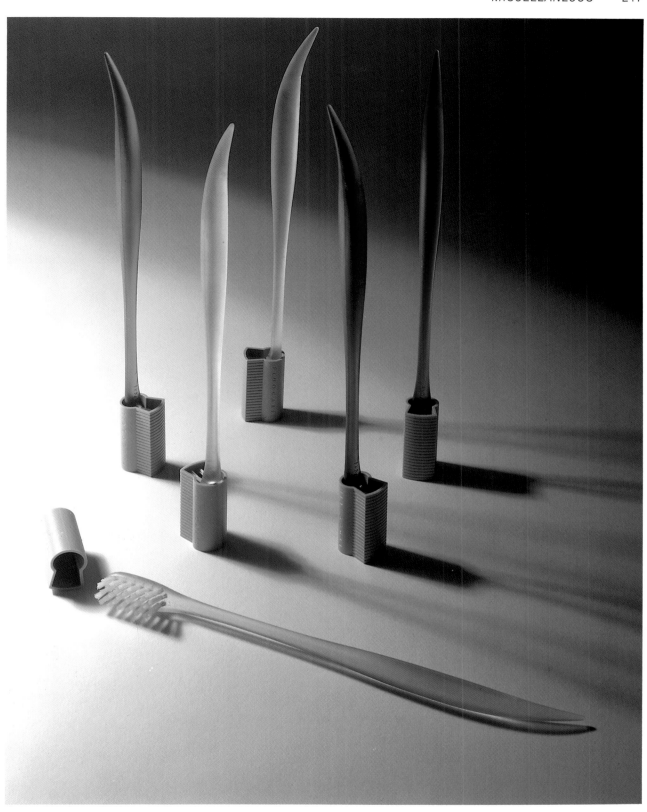

PRODUCT

**Fluocaril Starck Travel
Toothbrush**

DESIGNER

Philippe Starck

MANUFACTURER

**Laboratoires
Pharmaceutiques Groupil
S.A., France**

PHOTOGRAPHER

Gail Molina

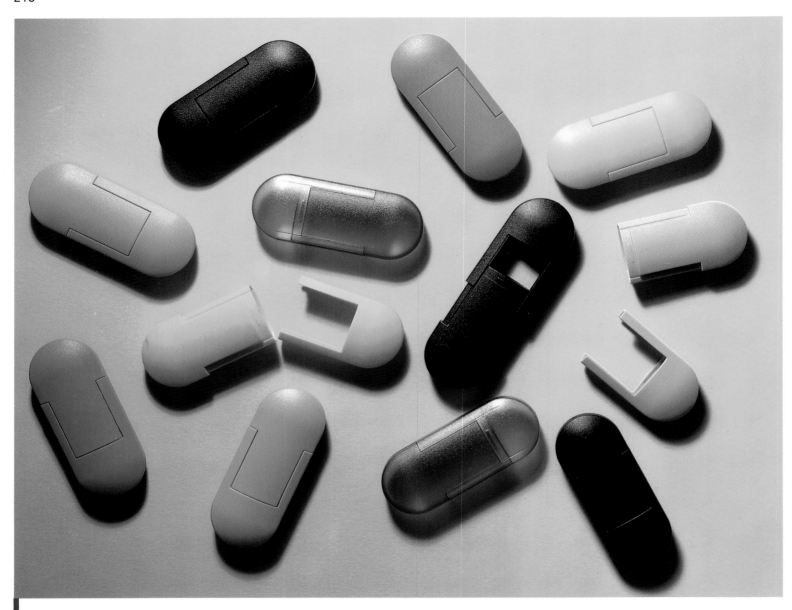

PRODUCT
Urban Spa Condom Case
DESIGNER
**Wharmby Associates,
England**
MANUFACTURER
**WAG Products LTD.,
England**
PHOTOGRAPHER
Gail Molina

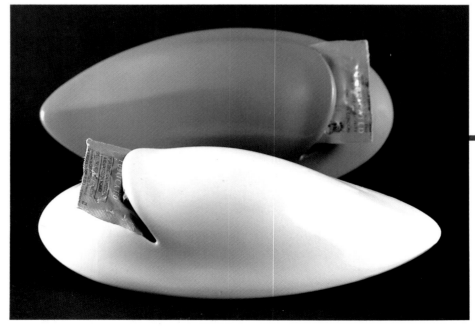

PRODUCT
SAFE Condom Keeper
DESIGNERS
**Lisa Krohn, Aaron Lown,
1992**
MANUFACTURER
Designers
PHOTOGRAPHER
Designers

PRODUCT

Hand Mirror

DESIGNERS

Laura Handler, David Peschal—Handler James Gager, Senior Vice President and Creative Director—Prescriptives Worldwide

MANUFACTURER

Prescriptives

PRODUCT

SPACECAB Medicine Cabinet

DESIGNERS

John von Buelow, Mark Andersen

MANUFACTURER

ZACA Inc.

PHOTOGRAPHER

Terry Sutherland

PRODUCT
Inax Urban Toilet
DESIGNER
GK Sekkei Incorporated
MANUFACTURER
Inax Corporation

PRODUCT
Zaza
DESIGNER
Masayuki Kurokawa
MANUFACTURER
Toto Ltd.
PHOTOGRAPHER
Mitsumasa Fujitsuka

PRODUCT
Serie Logica Mixer Tap
DESIGNER
Ramon Benedito
MANUFACTURER
Cia. Roca Radiadores
PHOTOGRAPHER
Joan Enric

PRODUCT
''Girotondo''
DESIGNER
Davide Mercatali
MANUFACTURER
Fantini
PHOTOGRAPHER
Zaccaria & Cortinovis

PRODUCT
InTouch Line
DESIGNERS
John von Buelow
S.G. Hauser
MANUFACTURER
Interbath
PHOTOGRAPHER
Terry Sutherland

PRODUCT
''Luna''
DESIGNER
Davide Mercatali
MANUFACTURER
Manital
PHOTOGRAPHER
Zaccaria & Cortinovis

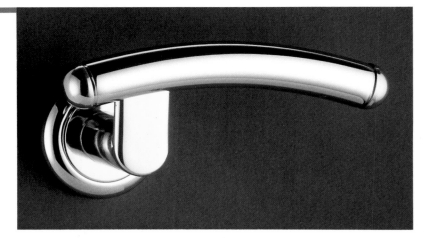

PRODUCT
''Spin'' Door Handles
DESIGNER
Makoto Komatsu
MANUFACTURER
**OHS/Japan
Representative in U.S.
Eastern Accent
International, Boston, MA**

PRODUCT
Musical Note Pulls
DESIGNER
**Frederic Schwartz,
Anderson/Schwartz
Architects**
MANUFACTURER
Aileron
PHOTOGRAPHER
Steve Moore

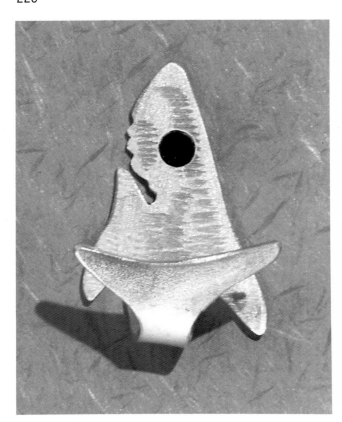

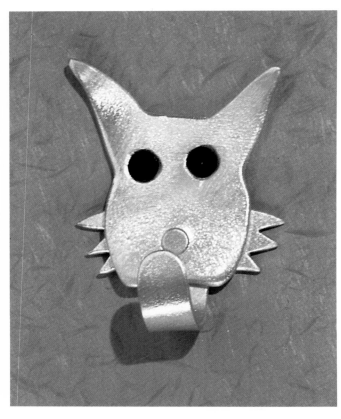

PRODUCT
"Animal Hooks"
DESIGNER
Patrick Moore
Available through
Archetype Gallery

PRODUCT
Animal Pulls
DESIGNER
Chris Collicott
MANUFACTURER
Chris Collicott
PHOTOGRAPHER
Chris Collicott

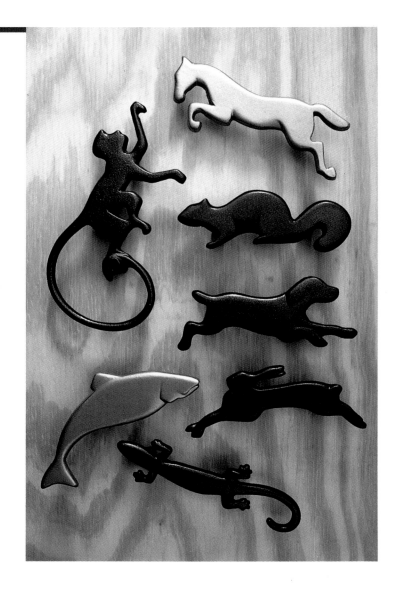

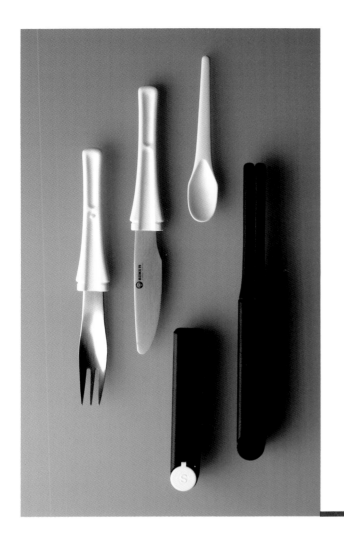

PRODUCT
ZAP Snac Pac
DESIGNER
Ernest Felix
MANUFACTURER
Heinrich Böker + Co.
PHOTOGRAPHER
Symmetrical

PRODUCT
Scissors
DESIGNER
Eric Chan, ECCO Design Inc.
MANUFACTURER
Alphax, Japan

PRODUCT

Armani Exchange Form

DESIGNER

James Geier and 555 Design Fabrication Management

MANUFACTURER

555 Design Fabrication Management

PHOTOGRAPHER

555 Design Fabriction Management

PRODUCT

Armani Exchange Coat Hanger

DESIGNER

James Geier and 555 Design Fabrication Management

MANUFACTURER

555 Design Fabrication Management

PHOTOGRAPHER

555 Design Fabriction Management

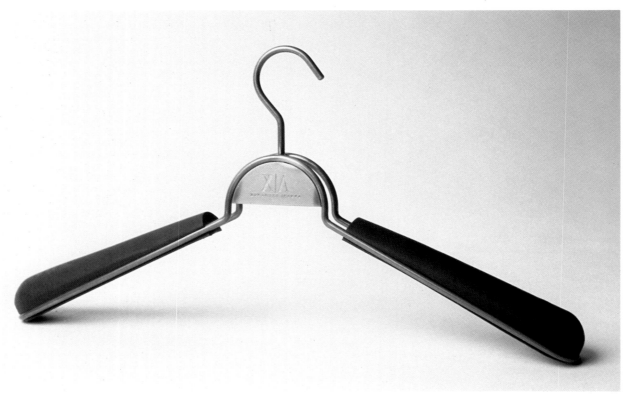

PRODUCT

Armani Exchange Basket

DESIGNER

James Geier and 555 Design Fabrication Management

MANUFACTURER

555 Design Fabrication Management

PHOTOGRAPHER

555 Design Fabriction Management

PRODUCT

Armani Exchange Costumer

DESIGNER

James Geier and 555 Design Fabrication Management

MANUFACTURER

555 Design Fabrication Management

PHOTOGRAPHER

555 Design Fabriction Management

PRODUCT

P + G

DESIGNER

Masayuki Kurokawa

MANUFACTURER

**Platinum Guild
International**

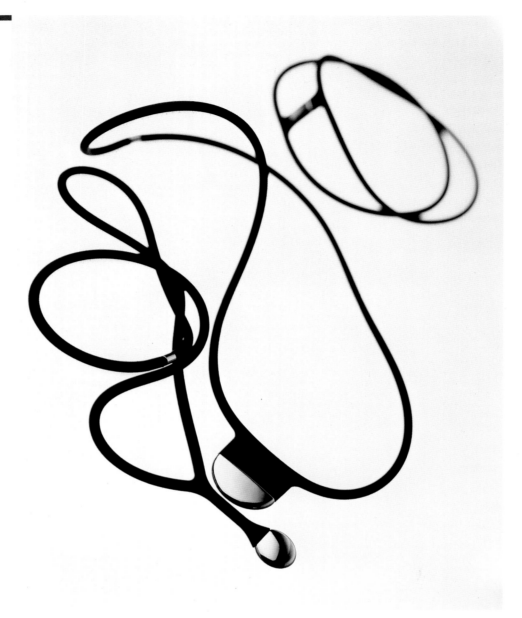

PRODUCT

**"Guardian Europe" Child
Safety Seat**

DESIGNERS

**Kenneth Grange, Johan
Santer—Pentagram Design
Ltd.**

MANUFACTURER

**Takata Corporation of
Japan**

PHOTOGRAPHER

Nick Turner (35mm only)

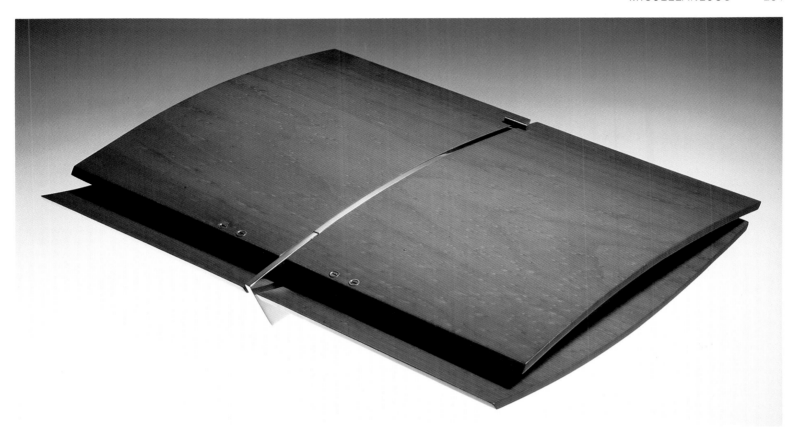

PRODUCT
Havanera
DESIGNER
Jaime Tresserra Clapes
MANUFACTURER
J. Tresserra Design SL

PRODUCT
Solar Blind
DESIGNERS
**Eric Chan, Jeff Miller—
ECCO Design Inc.**
MANUFACTURER
**Prototype by Ron Rezek
Lighting**

PRODUCT
Narita Express
DESIGNER
GK Incorporated
MANUFACTURER
East Japan Railway Co.

PRODUCT
**IBM Tucson
Inventor/Patent Display**
DESIGNERS
**John Acciaioli, Rick
Hodorowich**
MANUFACTURER
Designology, Inc.
PHOTOGRAPHER
Jeffry Muir Hamilton

555 Design Fabrication Management
1238 South Ashland Ave.
Chicago, IL 60608

A2Z
725 E. Hyde Park Blvd.
Inglewood, CA 90302

A/D
560 Broadway
New York, NY 10012

A & R Industrial Design
123 South Main St.
Royal Oak, MI 48067

Able Industrial
23 W. 35th St.
New York, NY 10001

Alpino
65 Gloucester Cres., Regents Park
London NW1 7EG, England

Anderson/Schwartz Architects
40 Hudson St.
New York, NY 10013

Apple
20525 Mariani Ave.
Cupertino, CA 95014

Archetype Gallery
137 Spring St.
New York, NY 10012

Annieglass Studio
303 Potrero St.
Santa Cruz, CA 95060

Artemide Inc.
1980 New Highway
Farmingdale, NY 11735

Asahi Optical Co., Ltd.
2-36-9 Maenocho
Itabashiku
Tokyo 134, Japan

Ashcraft Design
11832 W. Pico Blvd.
Los Angeles, CA 90064

B/Futch & Associates
1002 Wellstone Circle
Apex, NC 27502

Becker Design Inc. (BDI)
14140 Q Parke Long Court
Chantilly, VA 22021-1649

Bieffe Di Bruno Ferrarese S.P.A.
Via Pelosa, 78
35030 Caselle Di Selvazzano
Padova, Italy

Brueton Industries
30-20 Thomson Ave.
Long Island City, NY 11101

California Medical Products, Inc.
1901 Obispo Ave.
Long Beach, CA 90804

Carleton Designs
1015A Greenwood Rd.
Elk, CA 95432

Cassina S.p.A.
Via Busnelli 1
I 20036 Meda (Mi) Italy

Chris Collicott
1151½ N. La Brea Ave.
Los Angeles, CA 90038

Christine Van Der Hurd
99 University Pl.
9th Floor
New York, NY 10003

Clodagh Design International
365 First Ave.
New York, NY 10010

Cousins Design
599 Broadway
New York, NY 10012-3235

Dakota Jackson, Inc.
306 East 61 St.
New York, NY 10021

Dale Broholm Co.
15 Framan Rd.
Wellesley Hills, MA 02181

Isao Hosoe Design
Via Voghera 11
20144 Milano, Italy

Daskas Amsterdam
Brouwersgracht 1-3
1015 GA Amsterdam, The Netherlands

David Shaw Nicholls Corp.
55 Walker St.
New York, NY 10013

David Mercatali
Via Molino Delle Armi 45
20123 Milano, Italy

David Wiener Ventures
152 Hillspoint Rd.
Westport, CT 06880

Design Central
68 W. Whittier St.
Columbus, OH 43206

Design Board/Behaeghel & Partners S.A.
Avenue Georges Lecointe 50
1180 Brussels, Belgium

Design Inspiration
2505 Everett Ave.
Raleigh, NC 27607

Designhaus, Inc.
911 Western Ave.
Seattle, WA 98104

Designology
7641 E. Gray Rd.
Scottsdale, AZ 85260

Designwerks
1642 Las Trampas
Alama, CA 94507

Designworks/USA
2201 Corporate Center Dr.
Newbury Park, CA 91320

Dialogica
484 Broome St.
New York, NY 10013

Disseny Industrial
Balmes 360, 3-R. 2-A
08006 Barcelona, Spain

Eastern Accent
237 Newbury St.
Boston, MA 02116

Ecco Design
89 Fifth Ave.
Suite 600
New York, NY 10003

Erco Leuchten GmbH
Brockhauser Weg 80-82
5880 Ludenscheid, Germany

Fitch RichardsonSmith
10350 Olentangy River Rd.
Worthington, OH 43285

Flos SPA
Via Moretto 58
Brescia, Italy

Forma
108 E. Hargett St.
Raleigh, NC 27061

Frank Hosick Design
P.O. Box H
Vashon Island, WA 98070

Fujie Textile Co., Ltd.
4-7-12, Sendagaya, Shibuya-Ku
Tokyo, Japan 151

Gaggenau USA
425 University Ave.
Norwood, MA 02062

Gallery of Functional Art
2429 Main St.
Santa Monica, CA 90026

GK Design Group
3-30-14 San - Ai Bldg. Toshima-Ku
Tokyo, Japan

Glass & Glass Inc.
3286 M St., N.W.
Washington, DC 20007

Goldsmith Yamasaki Specht
900 N. Franklin St.
Chicago, IL 60610

Gordon Randall Perry
121 West Third St.
New York, NY 10012

Gray Design
688 South Avenue 21
Los Angeles, CA 90031

Group Four Design
147 Simsbury Rd.
Avon, CT 06001

Handler
225 Varick St.
9th Floor
New York, NY 10014

Henry Dreyfuss Associates
423 West 55th St.
New York, NY 10019

Human Factors Industrial Design
575 Eighth Ave.
New York, NY 10018-3011

Iain Sinclair Ltd.
16 Connaught St.
London W2 2AG, England

IBM SSPD Tucson
9000 South Rita Rd.
Tucson, AZ 85744

Ideo Product Development
7/8 Jeffreys Pl.
Jeffreys St.
London NW1 9PP, England

Jasia Szerszynska
144 Haberdasher St.
London N1 6EJ, England

JB Cumberland & Associates
370 Lexington Ave.
Suite 1002
New York, NY 10017

K & I Smythe
97 Alamo Ave.
Berkeley, CA 94708

Kallemo AB
Box 605
S-331 26 Varnamo, Sweden

Kane Design Studio
570 Alabama St.
San Francisco, CA 94110

The Knoll Group
Westinghouse Blvd.
Gateway Center
Pittsburgh, PA 15222

Kosta Boda
S-360 52 Kosta
Sweden

Krohn Design
23 W. 35th St.
New York, NY 10001

Krueger International
1330 Bellevue St.
P.O. Box 8100
Green Bay, WI 54308-8100

Leybold A.G.
Bonnerstr.498, D-5000
Cologne 51, Germany

Lisa Krivacka
155 West 20th St.
Apt. 6K
New York, NY 10011

Lunar Design, Inc.
119 University Ave.
Palo Alto, CA 94301

M&Co.
50 West 17th St.
New York, NY 10011

M.I. Design
40 Bramley Rd.
Southgate, London N14 4HR, England

Maison DUPIN SA
Rue du Rhone 11
1211 Geneva 11, Switzerland

Mark Steiner Design
214 Pemberwick Rd.
Greenwich, CT 06831

Markuse Corporation
10 Wheeling Ave.
Woburn, MA 01801

Masayuk Kurokawa Architect & Associates
Flat Aoyama 101, 5-15-9
Minami-Aoyama Minato-Ku, Tokyo, Japan

Michael Clapper Design
18 Dug Rd.
Lansing, NY 14882

Michael Rowe
401½ Workshops
401½ Wandsworth Rd.
London SW8 2JP, England

Michaeli W. Young Associates Inc.
45-28 11th Street
Long Island City, NY 11101

Machineart
66 Willow Ave.
Hoboken, NJ 07030

Miesner Design
2633 34th Ave.
Oakland, CA 94601

NEOTU
133 Greene St.
New York, NY 10012

Neumeister Design, Munich
Von-Goebel-Platz 8
8000 Munchen 19, Germany

Noto-Zeus Collection
Via Vigevano 8
20144 Milano, Italy

Nova Biomedical
2000 Prospect St.
Waltham, MA 02254-9141

NUNO Corporation
5-17-1 Axis B-1 Roppongi Minoto-Ku
Tokyo 106, Japan

O.P.M. Design
3100 Airport Ave.
Santa Monica, CA 90405

Pentagram Design Limited
11 Needham Rd.
London W11 2RP, England

Peter Diepenbrock
21 Holden St.
Studio 308
Providence, RI 02908

PharmaDesign Inc.
30 Technology Dr.
Warren, NJ 07059

Philips International B.V.
Corporate Industrial Design
Building SX-P, P.O. Box 21
5600 MD Eindhoven, The Netherlands

Polivka Logan Design, Inc.
245 Aldrich Ave. N. #375
Minneapolis, MN 55405

Product Genesis Inc.
300 Bent St.
Suite 200
Cambridge, MA 02141

Public Domain
148 W. 16th St.
New York, NY 10011

Rallis India Ltd.
Rallifan Factory LBS Marg Mulund (W)
Bombay, 400 080 Maharajhtra, India

Renquist/Associates, Inc.
P.O. Box 081400
Racine, WI 53408-1400

The Richard Penney Group
568 Broadway
Suite 702
New York, NY 10012

Richard Snyder
Elmwood Rd.
South Salem, NY 10590

RKS Design
7407 Topanga Canyon Blvd.
Canoga Park, CA 91303

Roche Harkins, Inc.
17 Clinton Dr.
Hollis, NH 03049

Rogov Corporation
6162 Nancy Ridge Dr.
Suite 101
San Diego, CA 92121

Ruine Design Associates
250 West 27th St.
Suite 6A
New York, NY 10001

S.G. Hauser Associates
24009 Ventura Blvd.
Suite 200
Calabasas, CA 91302

Sabattini Argenteria S.P.A.
Via Don Capiaghi
2 - 22070 Bregnano, Italy

Section Five Design Ltd.
5506 Lake View Dr. Apt. D
Kirkland, WA 98033

Skip Abelson
217 Rennie Ave.
Venice, CA 90291

Sonet Agency
123 East 54th St.
Suite 9E
New York, NY 10022

Sonneman Design Group, Inc.
26-11 Jackson Ave.
Long Island City, NY 11101

Stanford University
248 Seale Ave.
Palo Alto, CA 94301

Sterling Marking Products Inc.
349 Ridout St. N.
London, Ontario, Canada NGA 4K3

Tandem Computers Inc.
10300 N. Tantau Ave., Loc 55-54
Cupertino, CA 95014-0708

Technology Design Inc.
108 Main St. Box 5725
Bellevue, WA 98006

TER MOLST
Cogitat Collection
Grote Heerweg 35
8791 Beveren-Leie, Belgium

Thomson Consumer Electronics
600 N. Sherman Dr.
Indianapolis, IN 46201

Tim Wells Furniture
20 Cricket Ln.
Freeville, NY 13068

Toby Russell
1 Arlington Cottages, Sutton Ln. W4
London 4HB, England

Tres Design Group, Inc.
1440 North Dayton St.
Chicago, IL 60622

Ulrica Hydman-Vallien
Afors 361 04
Eriksmala, Sweden

Umbra U.S.A. Ltd.
1705 Broadway
Buffalo, NY 14212

Via Design, S.A.
Provenca, 356 Pral. 1a
08037 - Barcelona, Spain

Winfried Scheuer MA RCA
53 Leinster Square
London W2 4PU, England

Winona Lighting
3760 West Fourth St.
Winona, MN 55987

Woka
A-1010 Wien I., Palais Breuner
Singerstrasse 16 Austria

Yamaha Corporation
10-1, Nakazawa-cho
Hamamatsu, 430 Japan

Zigguart
419 West G St.
San Diego, CA 92101

Zona Alta Projects
8491 NW 17 St.
Suite 113N
Miami, FL 33126

INDEX

Designers

Design Firms

Photographers